RACISM

KEY IDEAS
Series Editor: Peter Hamilton
The Open University

KEY IDEAS

Series Editor: PETER HAMILTON
The Open University, Milton Keynes

Designed to complement the successful *Key Sociologists,* this series covers the main concepts, issues, debates, and controversies in sociology and the social sciences. The series aims to provide authoritative essays on central topics of social science, such as community, power, work, sexuality, inequality, benefits and ideology, class, family, etc. Books adopt a strong individual 'line' constituting original essays rather than literary surveys, and form lively and original treatments of their subject matter. The books will be useful to students and teachers of sociology, political science, economics, psychology, philosophy, and geography.

THE SYMBOLIC CONSTRUCTION OF COMMUNITY
ANTHONY P. COHEN, Department of Social Anthropology, University of Manchester

SOCIETY
DAVID FRISBY and DEREK SAYER, Department of Sociology, University of Glasgow

SEXUALITY
JEFFREY WEEKS, Social Work Studies Department, University of Southampton

WORKING
GRAEME SALAMAN, Faculty of Social Sciences, The Open University, Milton Keynes

BELIEFS AND IDEOLOGY
KENNETH THOMPSON, Faculty of Social Sciences, The Open University, Milton Keynes

EQUALITY
BRYAN TURNER, School of Social Sciences, The Flinders University of South Australia

HEGEMONY
ROBERT BOCOCK, Faculty of Social Sciences, The Open University, Milton Keynes

RACISM

ROBERT MILES

R
ROUTLEDGE
London and New York

First published in 1989
by Routledge
11 New Fetter Lane, London EC4P 4EE
29 West 35th Street, New York, NY 10001

Typeset by LaserScript Limited, Mitcham, Surrey
Printed and bound in Great Britain by Mackays of Chatham PLC, Kent

British Library Cataloguing in Publication Data

Miles, Robert, *1950-*
Racism. — (Key ideas).
1. Racism
I. Title II. Series
305.8

Library of Congress Cataloging in Publication Data

Miles, Robert, *1950-*
Racism / Robert Miles.
 p. cm. — (Key ideas)
Bibliography: p.
Includes index.
1. Racism. 2. Social classes. I. Title. II. Series.
HT1521.M495 1989   88–18504
305.8—dc19   CIP

ISBN 0-415-01809-9

No author and no reader changes the meaning of words. The struggle of discourses changes their meanings, and so the combination in which we put words together matters, and the order of propositions matters: through these, whatever our intentions, words take on meaning.

Macdonell 1986: 51

It is one of the penalties of toying with the race-notion that even a strong mind trying to repudiate it will find himself making assumptions and passing judgements on the basis of the theory he declaims.

Barzun 1938: 44

Contents

Acknowledgements

First, I thank my colleagues in the Research Unit on Migration and Racism in the Department of Sociology at the University of Glasgow for their comments and criticisms of earlier drafts of this book. Bruce Armstrong, Paula Cleary, Anne Dunlop, Jackie Lamont, Diana Kay, Nello Paoletti, Vic Satzewich and Edelweisse Thornley all contributed to a most useful series of research unit seminars during 1987, in the course of which they all too often drew my attention to my ignorance and faulty logic.

Second, some of the arguments expressed here have an origin in my continuing research collaboration with colleagues elsewhere in Europe. In particular, I wish to thank Frank Bovenkerk, Kristin Couper, Moustapha Diop, Han Entzinger, Marjan van Hunnik, Francien Keers, Marel Rietman, Daniel Singer, Jeanne Singer-Kerel and Gilles Verbunt for their intellectual stimulation, hospitality and considerable sense of humour.

Third, I have benefited considerably from the comments and advice of Dave Frisby at the University of Glasgow and Marie de Lepervanche at the University of Sydney, although perhaps they do not realise it.

Fourth, I gratefully acknowledge financial support from the British Council, the Carnegie Trust for the Universities of Scotland, the EEC, and the University of Glasgow. A variety of grants and awards from these institutions facilitated a wide-ranging programme of research and teaching activities in Europe over the past few years which contributed in a multitude of ways to the writing of this book.

Of course, responsibility for what you will read rests solely with myself.

Robert Miles
Glasgow

Introduction

Like many sociological concepts, racism has an everyday use and many everyday meanings. It has become a key idea in daily discourse as well as in sociological theory. Like all other component elements of what Gramsci called 'common sense' (1971: 323-33), much of the everyday usage is uncritical. But the concept has a peculiarity in so far as it is heavily negatively loaded. Thus, to claim that someone has expressed a racist opinion is to denounce them as immoral and unworthy. In brief, racism is, in the late twentieth century, a term of political abuse. All this presents special difficulties for the social scientist who attempts to defend the use of the concept. Whatever definition is offered has significance not only for the scope and direction of academic work but also for wider political debate, as was demonstrated in the exchange between Banton and Rex in the late 1960s which dwelt in part on whether certain statements made by the British Member of Parliament, Enoch Powell, could be described as racist (Banton 1970, Rex 1970). A similar debate took place in Australia in the mid-1980s (Liffman 1985, Cope and Kalantzis 1985) in the light of claims about Asian migration made by a Professor of History at Melbourne University (Blainey 1984, Markus and Ricklefs 1985). Before commenting on this issue further, it is therefore particularly important to identify the objectives, limitations and structure of this book.

OBJECTIVES, LIMITATIONS AND STRUCTURE

The principal objective is to set out a case for the continued use of the concept of racism in sociological analysis. Some writers have responded to the changing and varying usage of the concept by claiming that there is no longer any scope for finding it a place in theoretical discourse (Banton 1977: 156-72) while others use the concept without attempting to define it (CCCS 1984). This objective requires a historical review of the origin and usage of the concept, and a critical evaluation of recent attempts to theorise it. This is the agenda for the first two chapters. In the last two chapters, in the light of the critique offered of extant work, I set out an argument to justify and illustrate the continued usage of the concept in sociological analysis.

The analysis offered here has limits which are simultaneously geographical and historical. With certain exceptions, the historical analysis is confined to the period from the fifteenth to the twentieth century (although this is an ambitious time scale). This period is dominated by the emergence and domination of the capitalist mode of production. Within this historical restriction, a spatial limit is applied and I am concerned largely with racism in the 'western world'. This follows from the fact that the existing world capitalist system has its origin, in part, in the expansionary, trading activity of merchant capital based in Western Europe from the fifteenth century (Marx 1972: 323-37, Wallerstein 1974, Fox-Genovese and Genovese 1983). This gave way to colonial settlement and domination, and the subsequent incorporation of various parts of the world in an emergent capitalist system which until the early twentieth century was centred in Europe and specifically, although not exclusively, in Britain. The history of British colonialism therefore determines to a significant degree the geographical parameters of what follows. Included in these parameters are Western Europe, North America, parts of Africa and the Caribbean, the Indian subcontinent and Australasia.

These limitations imply some form of historical correlation between the emergence and development of capitalism and of racism. Indeed, such a correlation can be established although, as all statisticians know, a correlation is not in itself a measure of dependent determination. Statistical correlations may be spurious and, in the absence of additional evidence of determination, should be assumed to be so. The nature of the articulation between capitalism and racism is a subject for discussion elsewhere in the book.

I begin with a historical account of the emergence and genesis of European discourses about the Other. This is largely descriptive in content (the analytical problem of definition being left for discussion in chapter 2), identifying the early characterisation of non-Europeans in the pre-capitalist era, and proceeding to review the changing perceptions that accompanied the growth of merchant and industrial capital. The emergence of the idea of 'race' marks an important transition, followed later by the ascription of this idea with a biological content and by the 'scientific' legitimation of a biological hierarchy. Although subsequent scientific work exposed the falsity of these arguments, the idea of 'race' remains, and some 'scientists' continue to claim a biological or genetic substance to it. More recently, politicians have ascribed a 'natural' reality to what they identify as the consequences of 'racial difference'.

In chapter 2, I consider the analytical problem of definition, partly in the light of the preceding historical evidence, and partly in the light of more recent theoretical arguments which have, in various ways, enlarged the conceptual and explanatory scope of the concept. The essence of the latter development is that the concept of racism has come to be used to refer not only to imagery and assertions, but also to practices, procedures and outcomes, often independent of human intentionality and a specific ideological content. I argue that this conceptual inflation raises more problems than it resolves, and that the concept of racism should be used to refer only to what can broadly be called an ideology. In that context, I shall discuss the difficulties involved in identifying the parameters of such an ideology.

Having established a concept of racism, I go on in chapter 3 to explore more closely the nature of racism as a process of signification. I argue that racism 'works' by attributing meanings to certain phenotypical and/or genetic characteristics of human beings in such a way as to create a system of categorisation, and by attributing additional (negatively evaluated) characteristics to the people sorted into those categories. This process of signification is therefore the basis for the creation of a hierarchy of groups, and for establishing criteria by which to include and exclude groups of people in the process of allocating resources and services. The way in which racism 'works' has certain similarities with other discourses, and hence I comment on the interrelationship between racism, nationalism and sexism.

The objective of chapter 4 is to contextualise racism as a process of signification. Processes of signification occur in a material and historical context as component elements of allocative and exclusionary mechanisms. For example, beliefs about the specific attributes of a group derived from the signification of some physical characteristic play a significant role in allocating individuals to particular economic positions and in excluding them from receiving certain economic rewards and political rights. I explore the changing nature of these allocative and exclusionary processes in a number of different historical contexts and as a dimension of the historicity of capitalist development.

RACISM AS A POLITICAL QUESTION

This academic agenda warrants contextualisation. Within the western world in the late twentieth century, only small minorities of people voluntarily and positively describe themselves as racists. There is an official consensus that those who express racist beliefs and/or act in accordance with such beliefs should be condemned on the grounds that those beliefs are scientifically discredited and that they lead to human behaviour which is morally unacceptable. This consensus is grounded in a number of historical events which are widely known in the public domain: for example, the slave trade organised by merchant capital in a number of European nation states between the sixteenth and nineteenth centuries; the murder of some nine million Jews under the direction of the Fascist government in Germany between 1933 and 1945; the segregation practised in the United States from the late nineteenth century to the 1960s; the construction and maintenance of apartheid in South Africa. All of these events have led to the death of large numbers of people, and all have been legitimated to various degrees by racism.

This consensus may have begun to break down in Western Europe (and elsewhere) since the 1970s. Political parties expressing demands and policies which are not unlike those of Fascist groups in the 1930s have gained political representation in national and supranational parliaments (for example, Husbands 1981, Ogden 1987). And there has been a growth of violence against certain populations within Western Europe, often legitimated by claims that the victims are in some way or another inferior (EEC 1986). But these explicit expressions of racism have not occurred in a vacuum. Despite protestations of opposition to racism, a wider range of organisations and institutions, including the state itself, have actively and passively discriminated against minority populations. And these same populations have been shown to be disproportionately represented amongst those in low paid manual work, the unemployed, and those living in poor quality housing. The suspicion, if not the claim, is that this is due to widespread practices of exclusion motivated or legitimated by racism.

Additionally, from amongst the populations which have been the objects of racist agitation and exclusion there have emerged groups committed to engage in struggle to highlight and resist the consequences of racism (for example, ALTARF 1984). They have exposed the contradiction between the official consensus and the actual practice, and they have played a major role in placing the issue of racism on the political agenda. They have been joined by other sections of population in Western Europe concerned about the rise of Fascist parties and the increase in racist violence, but also about other, less obvious manifestations of racism. Together, they constitute in a broad sense an anti-racist movement, although there is often considerable disagreement amongst the groups involved concerning both means and objectives. Thus, the historical legacy and contemporary political practice interact in order to focus public attention on the unfavourable treatment and position of certain groups of people. Both in order to ensure that such events as the holocaust are never repeated and to relieve economic and political disadvantages, a moral and political appeal is made for an active commitment to anti-racism.

The concept of racism is therefore the object of political and ideological struggle. In this context, it will be argued in some quarters that the writing of another academic book is the least important task when there are so many other, more practical, objectives to be achieved. But the academic project cannot be dismissed in so facile a manner. Not only are there people in educational institutions wishing to learn about the nature and origin of racism, but the claims and objectives of the somewhat amorphous anti-racist movement cannot themselves go unquestioned when unwarranted assertions are made about the beast that is to be vanquished. As has been said on countless occasions concerning the unity of theory and practice, if the analysis is wrong, then it is likely that the political strategy will not achieve the intended objectives. Hence, I make no apology for this product of 'armchair reflection'. I am not ignorant of the nature and course of the struggles that have occurred, nor unaware of the necessity of recognising that the academic is a participant member of various social collectivities, and the consequent responsibilities that follow. I offer the book as an expression of my own committed opposition to racism, without apology or reservation.

This claim may be questioned on at least two counts. First, many, including those who articulate racism, will regard this explicit expression of commitment as evidence of political bias. But, as I demonstrate in the following pages, the claims of the racists have been successively contradicted by scientific evidence. Indeed, in a number of notorious instances, the proponents of racism have been shown to have consciously or unconsciously falsified their evidence in order to claim 'scientific' support for their arguments (Gould 1984). But even if it were true that the world's population is permanently divided into some form of biological hierarchy, the political case against unequal treatment which denies a common humanity remains. It is that all people should have the human right to live in economic and political circumstances that permit the full realisation of their faculties and abilities. This has been denied on the slave ships and plantations, in the concentration and death camps, under the Reserve and migrant labour system, and in all circumstances where the law is used to segregate and disadvantage particular populations. This bourgeois right (its existence is grounded in the dual emergence of capitalism and individualism) deserves to be defended, although it is also necessary to consider the extent to which this right can be fully realised within the framework of a capitalist society.

The second objection will come from those who maintain that racism is a 'black' experience which the 'white' person is unable to understand. This view is often defended with the claim that racism is an exclusive creation of, and an essential feature of, European, 'white' cultures and societies, and that all those who belong to those cultures and societies are therefore necessarily tainted with racism. It follows that 'white' people are themselves the origin or cause of the problem, and therefore that 'white' people lack the capacity to understand, analyse and explain racism. It may also be argued that 'white' involvement in exposing and resisting racism is only further evidence of a racist and colonising mentality because it denies those who are the victims the space to act as autonomous beings on their own account. These arguments are articulated more in the political than in the academic arena, although an echo of the former is apparent in the latter, evident for example in the problematic category of 'white sociology' (CCCS 1984: 133-4).

I do not accept these arguments, at least not in their 'hard' form. As will be argued later, it is mistaken to limit the parameters of racism by reference to skin colour, because various 'white' groups have been the object of racism. Furthermore, the expression of racism is not confined to 'white' people. There is no doubt, for example, that many of the statements made by the American 'black' Muslim leader, Louis Farrakhan, warrant description as racism (see *Searchlight*, March 1986 and September 1987). More significant here is the suggestion that 'experience' is the central arbiter of the ability to investigate, to learn and to know. If this is interpreted in its 'hard' form, it founders on the logical ground that if racism is a prerogative of 'white' people, a unique product of their practice and experience, then it may be asserted that only 'white' people can understand its motives and origin. Moreover, if experience is the ultimate arbiter of what is known and can be explained, it seriously limits the investigation of the extent of discriminatory practice. British studies of the extent of such practice have shown that people of Caribbean and Asian origin in Britain experience discrimination as occurring less often than is suggested by actor testing (Smith 1977: 127-40). In other words, if the 'black' experience in Britain is used as the only significant measure of reality, one operates with a criterion of inquiry which substantially underestimates the extent of exclusionary practice.

It is true, for example, that the experience of people of Caribbean and Asian origin in Britain is often different from that of the 'indigenous' population in so far as sections of the latter articulate racism and practise discrimination. It is also true that acceptance of racist and colonial imagery can lead to closure of the space within which resistance to racism is formulated and practised by members of the 'indigenous' population. The mistake is to assume thereby that all Caribbean and Asian experience is different from that of the indigenous population and that all members of the indigenous population consistently engage in such acts of closure. It is a mistake because such assumptions inaccurately generalise about a socially constructed category on the basis of the experience of a sample in particular contexts, and because they deny a relative objectivity in order to advance an absolute subjectivity.

Thus, although (indeed, because) there are limits to the experience of many 'white' people when compared with 'black' people, there is no single truth about racism which only 'blacks' can know. To assert that the latter is so is, in fact, to condemn 'white' people to a universal condition which implies possession of a permanent essence which inevitably sets them apart. As Said has remarked in a manner of understatement (1985: 322), 'the notion that there are geographical spaces with indigenous, radically "different" inhabitants who can be defined on the basis of some religion, culture, or racial essense proper to that geographical space is ... a debatable idea.' Armed with the notion that truth is relative and negotiated (the latter condition including the utilisation of repeatable and verifiable methods of investigation), and hence with the assumption that one may advance claims which will be shown subsequently to be wrong, there is no reason to believe that the colour of one's skin naturally or inevitably prevents one from contributing to an understanding of the nature and origin of racism. Equally, and for the same reason, one can only succeed in that task if (in a society in which skin colour is signified) others with a different skin colour participate in the realisation of that objective.

The political struggle over the concept, as well as the extent, of racism has been joined more recently by the New Right. The wider motives and intentions of this political movement are of limited relevance in this context and have been discussed critically elsewhere (Levitas 1986, Gordon and Klug 1986). With respect to racism, their intervention is grounded in a concern about the perceived consequences of anti-racist initiatives within Britain, and in the case of the recent collection of essays edited by Palmer (1986), particularly within the British education system. The concern of Palmer and his colleagues is apparently three-fold. First, it is that anti-racism is now a hegemonic ideology and practice (Palmer 1986: 1-2) and that the 'race relations' lobby is 'the single most powerful interest group we now have' (Honeyford 1986: 44). Second, it is argued that anti-racism makes 'the attainment of harmonious inter-communal relations more difficult' because it encourages 'resentment and suspicion in the minds both of the ethnic minorities and of the indigenous population' (Levy 1986: 120-1). And, finally, it is argued that anti-racists fail fully to examine the available evidence and therefore advance their claims without adequate factual support (Marks 1986: 38). Indeed, one author claims that 'It cannot be politically healthy that so much of the literature on race relations in Britain is distorted in a way not much removed from systematic lying' (O'Keeffe 1986: 195).

Given this commitment to a full examination of the evidence, this collection of essays edited by Palmer is fundamentally flawed because all three concerns are advanced without any corroboration. Moreover, their concern is not with anti-racism *per se*. More generally, the enemy is identified as Marxism in so far as it is claimed that anti-racist initiatives are either directly grounded in, or refract, Marxist analysis which is presented a priori as a false and unacceptable analysis (Palmer 1986: *passim*, see, for example, Flew 1986: 18-19, 23, Honeyford 1986: 55). In fact, it is doubtful whether much of the writing that appears under the anti-racist banner warrants the designation of Marxism, not least because many of the writers have identifed

Marxism as Eurocentric (Sivanandan 1982, Robinson 1983) or outdated (Gilroy 1987: 18-19, 245).

Nevertheless, Palmer's book is of some interest in this context. This is because it correctly identifies and exploits two central weaknesses in some of the literature that advances an explicit anti-racist perspective, although to state this is not to assent to the conclusions that the contributors to Palmer's book draw. First, a number of the papers object to the increasing tendency to use the concept of racism in a loose and often undefined manner (for example, Flew 1986), an objection with which I concur. However, not one of Palmer's contributors engages in a serious and sustained review either of the development of the concept or of its current usage in the academic literature. In this sense, the quality of the critique does not rise above the status of polemic and politically motivated sophistry.

While few of Palmer's contributors seek to deny that racism (or prejudice as they sometimes prefer) is entirely absent from Britain, and while not one wishes to describe himself or herself as a racist or to advance an explicitly racist claim, some effort is expended on justifying arguments and practices which others would define as racist. Honeyford claims that 'a preference for one's own kind' is a 'universal tendency' (1986: 52). O'Keeffe claims similarly that 'preference is not prejudice' and suggests that there is nothing unacceptable about preferring to 'marry people of the same race' (1986: 190). This sounds innocuous, although one is alerted to its problematic character by the absence of any evidence to support the claim of universalism. By itself, the claim that it is 'natural' to prefer 'one's own kind' is not a racist claim, although there are reasons to doubt its veracity. But it is an explicit justification of a process of inclusion and therefore of exclusion: to prefer is to rank and to choose to value something or person or group, and therefore necessarily to preclude some other thing, person or group. What then matters in the context of the debate about racism are the criteria by which 'one's own kind' and therefore the Other are categorised, and hence simultaneously included and excluded, and an explanation offered for such inclusion and exclusion.

O'Keeffe reveals the problematic consequences of the argument about preference when he claims concerning 'the question of immigration of non-whites' that (1986: 191), 'it is absurd to deny that an established community has the right to define and defend its essential identity. At present, that essential identity includes whiteness.' Presumably, this justifies an immigration policy which is designed to prevent members of 'races' who are not 'white' from entering and settling in Britain because the presence of such people would have the undesirable consequence of destroying this supposed 'white identity'. In the light of the definition advanced later in this book, this is certainly a racist argument: O'Keeffe uses somatic or phenotypical criteria to categorise distinct populations, and attributes negatively evaluated consequences to the presence of 'non-white' people in Britain in order to justify their exclusion by an immigration law which is therefore intended to prefer 'whites'.

There is a second theme running through Palmer's book which also receives attention below. Several contributors object to arguments which explain any statistical pattern of disadvantage characterising the position of people of Caribbean and Asian origin in Britain as being the consequence of racism (for example, Marks 1986: 36). In part, the objection to such arguments returns to the matter of the definition of racism. But, in addition, the objection is, first, that it is mistaken to assume that a statisical correlation is by itself proof of causality; and, second, that the statistical homogenisation of people of Asian and Caribbean origin may obscure significant differences between them. Logically and empirically, both arguments are well founded, although I do not draw the same conclusion, that racism is therefore not a determinant of, for example, the underachievement of West Indian children in British schools (for example, Flew 1986: 20).

It is significant that in attempting to show that those engaged in anti-racist politics are no more than politically motivated agitators, the contributors to Palmer's book collectively ignore the vast bulk of evidence which demonstrates the nature and extent of racism and related exclusionary practices within Britain. To mention just three examples, these authors make no mention of the surveys which have demonstrated the widespread nature of exclusionary practices experienced by people of Asian and Caribbean origin (Daniel 1968, Smith 1977, Brown 1984); of the recently released evidence that shows how successive British governments in the late 1940s and early 1950s sought a method to prevent 'coloured' British subjects from the colonies or Commonwealth from exercising their legal right to enter and settle in Britain whilst allowing 'white' British subjects from the colonies or Commonwealth to retain that right (for example, Joshi and Carter 1984, Harris 1987); nor of the recent studies which demonstrated that racist views are widespread amongst, for example, the Metropolitan police and company managers responsible for recruitment (Smith, D.J. 1983, Jenkins 1986).

The argument of this book is not that racism and related exclusionary practices are a minor, even insignificant, determinant of the structural position and experience of racialised populations. Rather, it is that the influence of racism and exclusionary practices is always a component part of a wider structure of class disadvantage and exclusion; the real challenge is to contextualise the impact of racism and related exclusionary practices, partly to highlight the specificity of that impact and partly to demonstrate the simultaneous continuities in the class positions and experiences of (in the case of Britain) people of Asian and Caribbean origin and people of indigenous origin. In other words, in the light of the extensive evidence of the existence and impact of racism and related exclusionary practices, the task that remains is to unravel the different forms and levels of determination, the articulations between racism, sexism, and nationalism and the exclusionary practices which are derived from these ideologies, in the context of the reproduction of the capitalist mode of production.

CONCLUSION

If racism brutalises and dehumanises its object, it also brutalises and dehumanises those who articulate it. Racism is therefore simultaneously a mediation between human beings similarly and differentially located in a class structure and a denial of their humanity, even if that denial is unequal by virtue of the relations of domination and subordination implicit in the mediation. It is therefore a problem for all who live in a social context where it is articulated and where it sustains exclusionary practices. As a phenomenon of mediation, all who are witness to it necessarily have a (sometimes specific) role in its identification, explanation, condemnation, and elimination.

1

Representations of the Other

INTRODUCTION

Migration, determined by the interrelation of production, trade and warfare, has been a precondition for the meeting of human individuals and groups over thousands of centuries. In the course of this interaction, imagery, beliefs and evaluations about the Other have been generated and reproduced amongst all the participants in the process in order to explain the appearance and behaviour of those with whom contact has been established and in order to formulate a strategy for interaction and reaction. The consequence has been the production of 'representations' (cf. Moscovici 1981, 1982, 1984) of the Other, images and beliefs which categorise people in terms of real or attributed differences when compared with Self. There is, therefore, a dialectic between Self and Other in which the attributed characteristics of Other refract contrasting characteristics of Self, and vice versa. The first intention of this chapter is to describe the content of these images, beliefs and evaluations which I shall collectively refer to as 'discourse' (Macdonell 1986: 1-4, Potter and Wetherell 1987: 7).

However, I am not concerned with all instances of interaction and discourse. For the reasons already stated, I focus specifically on representations generated within the western world about populations elsewhere, although this emphasis does not imply a denial that wherever groups have met, they have both responded with images, beliefs, and evaluations about the Other, and about the consequences of the presence of the Other (see Dickason 1984: 22-5). For example, within the Islamic world, there has been a representation of the populations that lived beyond its boundaries which focused specifically upon religion as the means to identify the Other (Lewis 1982: 64). Additionally, those populations with whom contact was established by European merchant capitalists, some of whom were later colonised, represented the European merchants, soldiers and administrators in drawings, paintings and carvings, as well as in the written word, and on a variety of artefacts. Often these images were stereotypical or represented the Other in terms of their own physical and cultural norms (Volkenkundig Museum Nusantara 1986). Finally, European explorers and missionaries report the fascination and, often, fear expressed by certain groups in Africa on their first contact with a person of European origin. One particular feature of Europeans that was reported as exciting interest was their skin colour (Cole 1972: 64, Hibbert 1984: 48, 62, 89, 101, 146).

The consequences of the European presence were also articulated by those who were its object, and in a manner which reflected the different experience and mode of existence of the colonised. In this literary example, André Brink constructs the following evaluation 'thought' by a descendant of the African population enslaved by the Dutch settlers:

> We of the Khoin, we never thought of these mountains and plains, these long grasslands and marshes as a wild place to be tamed. It was the Whites who called it wild and saw it filled with wild animals and wild people. To us it has always been friendly and tame. It has given us food and drink and shelter, even in the worst of droughts. It was only when the Whites moved in and started digging and breaking and shooting, and driving off the animals, that it really became wild. (Brink 1983: 21)

With this particular focus, my second intention is to demonstrate a shifting content and evaluation of the Other. Not all elements of representation change over time, but the combination of elements does not remain static. And although certain representations may be dominant in any one period, they do not necessarily remain unchallenged. Hence because imagery and belief change over time, it is necessary to chart the historicity of representations.

The recognition of this dynamic element in western representations of the Other is the prelude to understanding a significant transformation in the method of European representation. Thus, and third, I demonstrate the emergence of the use of scientific criteria to evaluate the Other. This epistemological break introduced new, universalistic criteria of measurement and assessment, and a measure of truth which led to a new status being attributed to western representations. It is now clear that these 'scientific' assessments of the Other were mistaken. However, many of the ideas that they give rise to have not been eradicated, but continue to structure common-sense discourse about the Other.

These objectives have to be set against a limit on the scope of what follows. I do not claim to offer a comprehensive analysis of western representations of the Other, only significant instances which illustrate these stated objectives. Contact between what we now know as the populations of European nation states and people from other parts of the world has a history of some thousands of years and any systematic analysis would require a text longer, and very different, from what is offered here. Hence many of my examples are drawn from the history of British colonialism. Moreover, I terminate this analysis at the end of the Second World War, for reasons that will become apparent in chapter 2.

BEFORE EUROPEAN EXPANSION

Many writers concerned with the history of European representations of the Other either begin their analysis with the period of European expansion and colonisation of the Americas (for example, Sivanandan 1973), or devote only limited attention to it (see Cox 1970: 322-32). They focus on the discourse about the populations of Africa, and the Americas that Spanish, Portuguese, French, English and Dutch explorers and merchants generated but thereby they ignore the links with earlier representations. European explorers and traders of the sixteenth and seventeenth centuries did not set out without expectations of the characteristics of the peoples they would meet. Rather, they occupied class positions in feudal societies which had a long tradition of imagining the Other, partly as a consequence of the experience of direct contact. Thus, for example, the African was represented in European thought long before European involvement in the slave trade (Walvin 1973: 2-7, Jordan 1968: 6, Walvin 1986: 69-72).

It should also be noted that earlier representations were created and reproduced in a politico-spatial context wherein Europe as it is known and exists today was absent. The economic and politial domination of north west Europe is historically specific and, prior to the fifteenth century, the geographical region that is now Europe had been subject to a variety of invasions from Asia (Baudet 1976: 4) and the 'old continuous nations' of Europe were haltingly emergent rather than extant (Seton-Watson 1977: 21-87). The notion of Europe as an entity began to emerge only in the eighth century (Lewis 1982: 18) and, until at least the twelfth century, it was subordinate to the economic and politico-military power of the Islamic world, its populations being in practice colonised (Kaye 1985: 61). Indeed, it was because the Islamic world constituted a dominant force, motivated and legitimated by a view of history by which 'the Muslims were the bearers of God's truth with the sacred duty of bringing it to the rest of mankind' (Lewis 1982: 39), that a representation of Europe as a distinct entity expressed by the common religion of Christianity was to emerge.

Moreover, the European regions which achieved economic and politico-military significance prior to the fifteenth century were around the Mediterranean rather than in north west Europe. Before then, the regions that are now Italy and Greece established and maintained a dominant economic and cultural position, sustained partly by military means. These were class societies, built largely upon the use of slave labour (Finley 1980: 67-92), and the imperialistic activities of their ruling classes brought them into contact with other populations throughout Europe and parts of northern Africa. Contact and interaction occurred in different arenas. The most important were in connection with travel, trade and military activity. Travellers' accounts supplied information about populations which were identified as culturally and physically different, while trade and military activity (including the occupation of parts of Africa) ensured more extensive and direct forms of contact.

In the context of a growing knowledge of the geographical extent of human existence, there developed in Greco-Roman thought an idea of the unity of the human species. A conception of human diversity, spatially dispersed, but bound together by the possession of characteristics that distinguished human beings from both gods and animals, existed and was transformed in various ways over five centuries, although it did not seriously challenge the continuity of a complex of class and sexual divisions within Greco-Roman society (Baldry 1965: 24-5, 122, 198-203). Moreover, it did not eliminate a conception of the existence of 'barbarians' beyond the borders of Greco-Roman society. The barbarian as Other was seen to lack the capacities of intelligible speech and reason, capacities that were considered to be the quintessence of Greco-Roman culture, even though they were recognised as human beings (Baldry 1965: 21-2, 143).

In the light of the expansion of the Greco-Roman empire into Africa, and of the subsequent representations of Africans within European culture, it is relevant to enquire about the nature of the discourse about the African in this complexity of ideas. These were representations also grounded in the direct experience of an African presence in Mediterranean Europe. Africans captured in military conflict were enslaved like all other prisoners of war. Others became, in effect, mercenaries. Additionally, Africans travelled to and were resident in the Greco-Roman world for educational and for diplomatic and commercial purposes (Snowden 1970: 121-2, 186, 1983: 33). How were Africans represented within Greco-Roman societies in the light of this interaction?

First, Africans were identified using certain physical features, notably skin colour but also hair type and nose shape (Snowden 1970: 2-5, 1983: 7). In addition, there was a definitive colour symbolism within Greco-Roman culture, by which whiteness was positively evaluated and blackness negatively evaluated. Blackness was associated with death and a conception of an underworld (Snowden 1983: 82-3). But the characterisation of Africans as having a black skin and the negative evaluation of blackness did not cohere to sustain either a negative stereotype or to constitute a legitimation of slavery (Davis 1984: 33). Rather, and second, Africans were identified generally as human beings with the capacity for freedom and justice, piety and wisdom (although some conceptions included elements of idealisation and unreality). They were also respected as warriors and soldiers (Snowden 1970: 181, 1983: 55-9, 68). And although some writers associated beauty with whiteness, there was also a widely held assumption that the criteria of beauty were subjective. Indeed, other writers extolled blackness as beautiful (Snowden 1983: 63, 76).

Third, there was speculation about the origin of the phenotypical and cultural differences that were identified as signifying difference. The dominant explanation in the Greco-Roman world was environmental in nature, the argument being that human physical appearance and cultural variation were determined by climatic, topographical and hydrographical conditions (Baldry, 1965: 50). This argument was used to explain the whole range of phenotypical diversity that was known at that time. For example, concerning Africans, it was suggested that skin colour and hair type were the product of constant exposure to the hot sun (Snowden 1970: 172-3, 1983: 85-7).

In addition to the representations of the African as an *experienced* Other (in the sense that there was direct contact and interaction with certain African populations) there were also representations within Greco-Roman thought of an *imagined* Other (in the sense that the representations had, in fact, no empirical reality, although that was not how these representations were experienced at the time). That the boundary between the experienced and the imagined Other is an artificial one in the Greco-Roman frame of reference is made evident in the *Natural History* of Pliny the Elder; this text included a primarily (although not an exclusively) phenotypical typology of populations, many of which were given a particular spatial location in the world, mainly in Africa, India, and the region of the Caucasus. This typology included Ethiopians, although their spatial location was imprecise, and also *Cynocephali, Blemmyae, Anthropophagi, Sciopods*. These populations were attributed with various physiological and cultural characteristics: the *Cynocephali* were dog-headed humans and the *Sciopods* had a single, very large foot, while the *Anthropophagi* were represented as eaters of human flesh (Friedman 1981: 8-21).

This typology, and associated representations and explanations, was expanded and modified by other writers and passed into the subsequent medieval European literary tradition. Within this tradition, a causal relationship between physical appearance, moral character and spatial location was asserted and, as in Greco-Roman thought, climate was considered to be a major independent determinant, but the three-fold climatic division of Greek thought was expanded (Friedman 1981: 52). Additional transformations occurred, the most significant being the religious meanings attributed to these representations. Within the Greco-Roman world, natural events considered to be indicators of God's intentions towards human beings were defined as *portenta* or *monstra*. Initially, *monstra* defined unusual individual or anomalous births, but its meaning was extended through the Middle Ages to include whole populations of people supposedly characterised by anomalous phenotypical characteristics, although the sense of divine warning remained (Friedman 1981: 108-16).

This premonitory meaning was subsequently transformed into one of punishment as Christianity became the prism through which all knowledge about the world was refracted, and as a result of which a literal Biblical explanation for the material world predominated. Consequently, the problem was to explain the nature and origin of these *monstra* in a way that was consistent with the Biblical representation of history. Concerning their nature, the issue was whether or not they were human, a crucial matter which determined whether or not they could be the object of missionary activity and conversion (Friedman 1981: 178-80). It was also necessary to explain the origin of these *monstra*. One explanation advanced by medieval European writers was that they were part of God's creation plan, the purpose of which had yet to be revealed. Others argued that one or a group of Adam's descendants had induced God's wrath, as a result of which their descendants had been physically disfigured and exiled to the periphery of the world. This explanation accepted a single origin of humanity as set out in the Bible but accounted for the subsequent diversity in human form. While the latter remained a subordinate explanation for a long period, it received increasing expression and support during the course of the medieval period (Friedman 1981: 88-103) and came to play a major ideological role in the period of European expansion. The consequence was an association between the Other *qua monstrum* and sin.

We have seen that various human physical features (some imaginary) were signified as monstrous, one of which was skin colour. Western Christianity associated certain colours with a range of additional meanings, with the result that it embodied a colour symbolism mirroring that of the preceding classical world. A white/black contrast expressed a complex of additional meanings, similarly dichotomous, such as good/evil, pure/diabolical, spiritual/carnal and Christ/Satan (Bastide 1968: 36). Thus colour expressed a hierarchical, religious evaluation which attained a more widespread secular content within Western culture (Gergen 1968: 119), parallels with which can be drawn with the Islamic world (Lewis 1971, Davis 1984: 32-51). Where distinctions between human beings were designated by reference to skin colour, this colour symbolism had a powerful evaluative implication. Monstrousness, sin, and blackness therefore constituted a rather different form of Trinity in European Christian culture in this period.

Thus, in medieval Europe, there was a discourse of the Other as a phenotypical and cultural deviant from a norm which was established by the represented characteristics of European writers. This Other took a plurality of monstrous forms, some of which were purely imaginary while others were derived, in part, from empirical observations of non-European peoples. Within late medieval European literature, a representation of the wild man emerged:

> This creature possesses many of the features of earlier monstrous peoples – hairiness, nudity, the club or the branch – features that imply violence, lack of civilised arts, and want of a moral sense. The wild man is usually shown in a wooded setting, far from the abode of normal men. (Friedman 1981: 200, also Dickason 1984: 70-80)

In particular, the wild man was attributed with an aggressive and untamed sexuality, the female form being represented as a seductress of ordinary men (White 1972: 21-2). The wild man therefore represented the opposite of the ideal Christian life. 'He is desire incarnate, possessing the strength, wit and cunning to give full expression to all his lusts' (White 1972: 21). His condition was thought to be the result of the abolition of social convention and control, and an inevitable punishment for anyone who submitted to desire (White 1972: 30).

As far as the European feudal ruling classes were concerned, this image marked the boundary of the known and 'civilised' world, a boundary that in the medieval period encompassed Europe and parts of Africa and Asia. The arena within which this image circulated was later expanded by the search of several European feudal ruling classes for new trade routes and, thereby, the 'discovery' of the 'new world'. As a result, the content of the Plinian typology was increasingly challenged by the accumulation of observations arising from travellers' accounts of the populations that they had met. Neither merchants nor pilgrims reported the presence of *Sciopods* or *Cynocephali*, but a representation of the Other remained.

EUROPE AND THE ISLAMIC WORLD

Before the interests of the feudal monarchies and merchant capital of Western Europe combined in order to colonise the Americas from the fifteenth century onwards, the main focus of external interest (and concern) was the Middle

East, North Africa and India, collectively known as the Orient. Hence, Daniel has observed that 'Europe's idea of the "foreigner" was based for many formative centuries exclusively on the Arab world' (1975: 322). Thus, not only did Europeans create a discourse of an imagined Other at the edge of European civilisation, but they created a discourse of a real Other represented as a result of conflicting material and political interests with a population which came to mark the boundary of Europe, not only spatially but also in consciousness.

In an emergent, feudal Europe wherein class domination was secured partly by means of Christianity, there was a heightened consciousness of the existence of Islam as a theology and of the dominance of Islam in lands within and in close proximity to Europe during the period from the mid-seventh century to the sixteenth century. The consequence was a definition of Islam and the Islamic world as the source of theological and political difficulties for Europe (Southern 1962: 3, 13). Spatially, the sustained point of contact between Europe and the Islamic world was the Mediterranean region, notably in Spain, but commercial contact, through trade, also occurred elsewhere in the Mediterranean and beyond (Daniel 1975: 109, 220, 229). During the early part of this period, the primary contact was with the Arab world, but by the fourteenth century, the Islamic 'threat' was increasingly thought to lie with the rise of the Ottomon Turks, although the form taken by the representation of the Islamic Other did not change substantially (Daniel 1975: 314-17). The image of the wild Saracen was replaced by that of the wild Turk, but within Europe both groups were seen as Muslims, and the discourse of Other that was constructed took this as the central focus.

The European image of Islam, and those who practised it, achieved a significant degree of coherence in the twelfth and thirteenth centuries, although a number of the key themes which recur over the centuries were evident much earlier (Daniel 1960: 275, 1975: 31-9). The Islamic Other was portrayed as barbaric, degenerate and tyrannical, and these alleged characteristics were considered to be rooted in the character of Islam as a supposedly false and heretic theology. The object of much of the attack was the prophet of Islam, Muhammad, who was represented as an imposter by claims that his life exemplified violence and sexuality (Daniel 1960: 78, 107). These were not portrayed as purely personal failings. It was argued that the theology that Muhammad created for his own ends embodied violence and sexuality, with the consequence that believers and followers of the theology inevitably behaved in similar ways. Thus Islam was portrayed as founded on, and as spreading itself by means of, aggression and war, and as permitting and encouraging polygamy, sodomy, and a general sexual laxity. It was argued that Islam reproduced the idea of the 'holy war' against all non-Muslims, in the course of which the latter would be either brutally murdered or enslaved, and a notion of Paradise as a garden of sexual delights and passions (Daniel 1960: 123-5, 136-54, 1966: 5, 1975: 234, 243).

The equation of Islam with violence was sustained by a clerical agitation that culminated in the eleventh century in what became known in Europe as the Crusades. Islamic occupation of the Holy Land was considered to be illegitimate, and was therefore viewed as evidence of aggression (Lewis 1982: 22). Hence, war against the Saracen to regain the Holy Land was justified theologically in the name of the Christian God. Islamic resistance to the European armies was interpreted as further evidence of an inherent tendency towards violence and cruelty, while identical acts of war by Christians were seen as means by which God could be glorified (Daniel 1960: 109-13, 1975: 111-39). It was not until the late seventeenth century that the Islamic world ceased to be perceived within Europe as an external threat (Harbsmeir 1985: 73).

In a context where the nature of the material world, and relations between people, were explained and structured through religion, European represent- ations of the populations of other regions were organised necessarily in terms of religion. Thus, the representation of the Other was a consistent distortion of Islam, grounded in an alternative theology, Christianity. Christian literature about Islam set out to

> establish that Muslim Arabs were different from Christian Europeans. This was expressed primarily in theological terms, because that is how the conformity of Europe was expressed. In a period when Europe was in a mood of aggression and expansion, its surplus energy created an attitude to its Arab and Arabic-speaking neighbours which was based, not on what the Arabs were like, but on what, for theological reasons, they ought to be like. (Daniel, 1975: 248)

The theological character of this representation of the Other was evident in the characterisation of Islam as the collective embodiment of, and the ultimate expression of, heresy.

In sum, 'Islam was seen as the negation of Christianity; Muhammad as an imposter, an evil sensualist, an Antichrist in alliance with the Devil. The Islamic world was seen as Anti-Europe, and was held in suspicion as such' (Kabbani, 1986: 5). The Other was represented in thought structurally in terms of a binary opposition, the axis of which was religious, and in terms of content, as backward, inherently cruel and violent and irrationally sexual (Said 1985: 167, 188, Kabbani, 1986: 6, 15, 41). The content of the representation within medieval Europe identifed the Other as intrinsically different, a conception simultaneously expressive and a reinforcement of the 'Self/Other' duality.

EUROPEAN EXPANSION AND COLONISATION

By the fifteenth century, the centre of economic and political power in Europe had consolidated in the emergent nation states of the north and west of the continent (Kiernan 1972: 12-13, Wallerstein 1974). Trade, travel, and exploration were interdependent elements in an attempt by the feudal ruling classes to resolve a major economic crisis (Fox-Genovese and Genovese 1983: 10) and together, they widened the European contact with populations elsewhere in the world. This resulted in a major change in the structural context within which representations of the Other were generated and reproduced. Up to this point, the non-Islamic Other was beyond and outside the European arena. Moreover, in the case of the discourse about the Islamic Other, it was for a long time a representation generated in the context of European subordination to a greater economic and military force.

But once the emergent European city and nation states began to expand their material and political boundaries to incorporate other parts of the world within a system of international trade (Braudel 1984: 89-174), a system which was subsequently linked with colonial settlement, the populations they confronted in this exercise were within the arena of Europe in an economic and political sense, even though not spatially. And when colonisation became an objective, a class of Europeans began a new era of contact and interrelationship with indigenous populations, a contact that was increasingly structured by competition for land, the introduction of private property rights, the demand for a labour force, and the perceived obligation of conversion to Christianity. Collectively, these were all embodied in the discourse of 'civilisation'.

The Europeans who travelled in pursuit (individually or in some combination) of trade, military advantage, religious mission, and curiosity carried with them expectations about what and whom they might meet which were derived from extant verbal and written accounts of the Other (for example, Dickason 1984: 18, 80). They came therefore with their own intentions and objectives which influenced their representations of those populations with whom they came into contact, and with a discourse of the Other, a discourse that was both sustained and extensively reworked. Thus, when Columbus 'discovered' the 'new world', he reported finding 'savage' but not 'monstrous' people (Friedman 1981: 198). Representations based on the empiricism of direct experience permitted a transformation in the content of the representation of the Other, but the existence of the Other as a mirror of what the European was not remained largely, although not exclusively, unquestioned.

Travellers' accounts of their experiences were an increasingly significant source of representations from the sixteenth century because the development of printing and the emergence of the book as a commodity (Febvre and Martin 1976: 180-97) permitted their wider, although still far from extensive circulation (Febvre and Martin 1976: 278-82). Travel books were published throughout Europe (Dickason 1984: 6-7) although they were most common and proved most popular in England (Curtin 1965: 10-14, Cole, 1972: 59-63). They were published for profit and, secondarily, to educate and entertain, and their intended 'mass' audience included the partially educated as well as the ruling class. Many were translations of texts published in other European languages, with the result that, for example, Iberian experiences and representations of Indian populations in the Caribbean and South America circulated in other European countries.

As representations of the Other, the travellers' sense of the normal served to identify the abnormal characteristics of the people with whom contact was established and of their mode of life. Hence, Curtin has observed regarding Africa 'the reporting often stressed precisely those aspects of African life that were most repellent to the West and tended to submerge the indications of a common humanity' (Curtin 1965: 23). A negative representation of the Other therefore served to define and legitimate what was considered to be the positive qualities of both author and reader.

One well-known English collection of travellers' reports from the period of European expansion is that edited by Richard Hakluyt (Febvre and Martin 1976: 281). It was first published in 1589-90 and a second enlarged edition, with the title *The Principal Navigations, Voyages, Traffiques and Discoveries of the English Nation*, appeared between 1598 and 1600. This was a collection dedicated to the demonstration of English superiority at sea.

> It cannot be denied, but as in all former ages, they have been men full of activity, stirrers abroad, and searchers of the most remote parts of the world, so in this most famous and peerless government of Her most excellent Majesty, her subjects, in compassing the vast globe of the world more than once, have excelled all the nations and people of the earth. (Hakluyt 1972: 33)

So how were the 'less excellent people of the earth' represented in these reports and other writings?

Non-European peoples were not represented in a homogenous manner, except in the most general sense of their being, by definition, less 'excellent' than the English. Those travellers who went east, into Russia and Central Asia, tended to describe the people that they met using the words 'barbarous', 'tyrant' or 'infidel' (Hakluyt 1972: 63, 80, 86, 123, 245). Rarely was any reference made to their physical appearance (see, for an exception, Hakluyt 1972: 101) and there were few remarks concerning their cultural practice. The discourse of tyrant and infidel reproduced that of the Islamic world generated earlier within Europe, and signified religion as the means by which to establish a dialectic between Self and Other.

But the travellers who sailed to the Americas, to Africa and India remarked consistently on the skin colour (and other physical characteristics such as hair type) of the indigenous populations and, although not exclusively, on their semi- or complete nakedness (Jordan 1968: 4, Cole 1972: 64-5, also Sanders 1978: 211-25). For example, John Hawkins commented on the people of West Africa

> The people of that part of Africa are tawny, having long hair without any apparel, saving before their privy members ... The 29 we came to Cape Verde. These people are all black, and are called negroes, without any apparel, saving before their privities: of stature goodly men. (Hakluyt 1972: 105-6)

Concerning the people he met on the South American mainland, he wrote

> These Indians being of colour tawny like an olive, having every one of them both men and women hair all black, and no other colour, neither men nor women suffering any hair to grow in any part of their body, but daily pull it off as it groweth. They go all naked, the men covering no part of their body but their yard, upon the which they wear a gourd or piece of cane, made fast with a thread about their loins, leaving the other parts of their members uncovered, whereof they take no shame. The women are also uncovered, saving with a cloth which they wear a hand-breadth, wherewith they cover their privities both before and behind. (Hakluyt 1972: 107-8)

Ralph Fitch represented the population of Ceylon as follows: 'Their women have a cloth bound about them from their middle to their knee: and all the rest is bare. All of them be black and but little, both men and women' (Hakluyt 1972: 267).

The populations of these parts of the world also tended to be represented as savages and/or cannibals (Dickason 1984). John Hawkins described Dominica as 'an island of cannibals' (in Hakluyt 1972: 107) and Thomas Cavendish wrote of a population on the South American mainland: 'In this river there are great store of savages which we saw, and had conference with them: they were men eaters, and fed altogether upon raw flesh and other filthy food' (Hakluyt 1972: 279). James Lancaster described the inhabitants of the Cape of Good Hope as 'black savages very brutish' (in Hakluyt 1972: 361), a view endorsed by seventeenth century travellers who described them as 'beasts in the skins of men' and as being halfway between man and ape (Novak 1972: 188). Whilst seeking the Northwest Passage, Martin Frobisher made contact with the people living in the northern polar region. He described them as fierce and cruel, and provided a lengthy description of their appearance and cultural practices, including the following assertions:

> They are men of a large corporature, and good proportion: their colour is not much unlike the sunburnt country man who laboureth daily in the sun for his living ... I think them rather anthropophagi, or devourers of man's flesh than otherwise: for that there is no flesh or fish which they find dead (smell if never so filthily) but they will eat it, as they find it without any other dressing. (Hakluyt 1972: 192-4)

The use of the term *anthropophagi* is an instance of the way in which Plinian categorisation shaped travellers' representations several centuries later and is consistent with the argument that the attribution of the cannibal label consistently occurs in Western representations of the Other (Arens 1979).

But references to savagery and cannibalism were not the only represent-ations that accompanied the signification of skin colour and nakedness. Columbus distinguished between *canibales* and *indios*; the latter he represented as exhibiting kindness and deference and as showing no evidence of bestiality (Sanders 1978: 93-4, 123-4). Francis Drake described the population of the island of Batjan in the Moluccas in the following manner:

> The people of this island are comely in body and stature, and of a civil behaviour, just in dealing, and courteous to strangers. The men go naked, saving their heads and privities, every man having something or other hanging at their ears. The women are covered from the middle down to the foot, wearing a great number of bracelets upon their arms. (Hakluyt 1972: 186)

Two English travellers to Virginia described the Indians that they met as 'most gentle, loving and faithful, void of all guile and treason, and such as live after the manner of the golden age' (in Hakluyt 1972: 274). Indeed, some people described as savages were described as 'harmless', as was the indigenous population of Newfoundland by Sir Humphrey Gilbert (in Hakluyt 1972: 236).

After initial contact more complex representations, which included positively evaluated elements, were constructed in the course of colonisation. For example, a respect developed for certain aspects of the life of the North American Indian, including their perceived strength and agility, and their hunting and fishing skills (Nash 1972: 68). In the case of the Carib Indians in the Caribbean, although they were represented as depraved by virtue of their alleged cannibalism, they were also attributed with the characteristics of courage and strength (Robe 1972: 45). For some observers, certain Indian populations were represented as a paradisiacal Other, as a population living in a condition of original harmony and egalitarianism, of absolute fulfilment (Baudet 1976: 26-8, 35-6). Thus the existence of non-Europeans was interpreted as a measure of the loss within Europe of an earlier 'golden age' or 'paradise' (cf. Popkin 1974: 129, Baudet 1976: 10-11). This discourse served to identify the observer as living in an unnatural, depraved condition, desirous of discovering the way to return to the ideal conditions that existed before the Fall. This supports the interpretation of those who have argued that the conception of the 'noble savage' existed long before Rousseau (Symcox 1972: 227-8, Baudet 1976: 11, Friedman 1981: 163-77, Dickason 1984: 59, 81).

But these positive representations have to be contextualised and it remains the case that the majority of descriptions in Hakluyt's collection of non-European peoples contain pejorative terms (cf. Friedman 1981: 164). In addition to the examples already cited, South American Indians were described as 'a warlike kind of people' and 'very ugly and terrible to behold' (Hakluyt 1972: 139), Indian Brahmins as 'a kind of crafty people, worse than the Jews' (1972: 259), the Javanese as 'heathen' (1972: 293), and the population of an island off the African coast as 'treacherous' (1972: 362). Hence, if there was no single representation, neither was there an equality of negative and positive meanings. The complexity of European representations was hierarchically ordered around the view that Europeans were superior by virtue of their 'civilisation' and achievements (of which world travel and trade were but one sign): the condition of the Other was represented as a proof of that interpretation.

In so far as the mythical nature of the Plinian and other categorisations was exposed by direct experience in the sixteenth and sevententh centuries, then that experience was neither universal nor uniform, and the consequent representations were multifaceted and therefore contested and contradictory. Nevertheless, these empirically based representations were not entirely novel for they contained transformations of earlier representations. For example, the images of the wild man and of monsters, with their long pedigree, both shaped and were reinvigorated by the European experience of contact with many of the indigenous populations of Africa, the Americas and even the polar regions (Friedman 1981: 203-4, Fryer 1984: 137). The untamed aggression, sexuality, and bestiality of the 'mythical' wild man previously located in the forested edges of (and within) Europe were given a more precise and specific geographical location in the new world. Moreover, this incarnation of the wild man was also distinguished by skin colour, permitting a conception of the Other as 'black' and therefore definitively distinct from the European who was 'white'.

In particular instances, the label *anthropophagi* was applied to certain groups, but in a new form. Columbus initiated the idea that those Indians who were named Caribs were, by custom, eaters of human flesh and, by a process of linguistic transformation, this name gave rise to the more familiar (in Western Europe) label 'cannibal'. Spanish explorers and colonisers in the Caribbean and Mexico increasingly applied the term to the peoples with whom they established contact, although in the written records of the period there is no first-hand witness account of the act of eating human flesh. The increasing utilisation of the term seems to correlate positively with indigenous resistance to the Spanish presence and practices of attempted military subjugation and the induction of indigenous peoples into unfree labour (Sanders 1978: 101, Arens 1979: 44-77).

Thus, direct contact and interaction with populations outside Europe was accompanied by a simultaneous reaffirmation and reconstruction of earlier representations (Walvin 1986: 72). With European discovery of what was Eurocentrically defined as the 'new world' (it was certainly not new to those populations who were living there), these representations increasingly refracted a new purpose as discovery was followed by settlement, and settlement by the introduction of systems of unfree labour (Miles 1987a) to exploit the natural resources initially for the benefit of the feudal ruling classes of Europe. Contact and interaction did not therefore occur in a neutral or equally balanced context. Rather, colonisation proceeded in a context of conflicting interests and unequal military resources, and was usually (although not universally) effected using various forms and degrees of direct force. The European classes involved in this process (re)constructed representations of these indigenous populations, both to legitimate their actions and in response to their experience of those populations. There was, as a consequence, a complex articulation between justification of class interests and strategies, and empirical observation in changing situations. The representations of the Other that resulted from this were neither absolutely homogeneous, nor static (for example, George 1958, Walvin 1986: 77), for the following reasons.

First, colonisation had neither a singular character nor a universal course. Bloody conflict, enforced labour and political subordination were common accompaniments of colonisation, as the examples of Central and North America and the Caribbean demonstrate (for example, Williams 1964: 3-29, Wolf 1982: 131-57), but other strategies were employed. In other contexts, mutually (although not equally) beneficial structures of accommodation and exchange predominated for at least certain periods of time, in the course of which the indigenous modes of production and accompanying social relations were maintained in a modified form, as happened in New Zealand and Canada (for example, Oliver 1981: 172, Wolf 1982: 158-94). Where the colonised collected or produced use values which could serve as commodities (as in the case of the Canadian fur trade) or where the colonised responded to the European presence by producing use values for the colonisers (often in the form of food), and where the colonised possessed knowledge and skills to permit survival in what the European coloniser experienced as a hostile natural environment, relations of interdependence were established.

In such circumstances, hostile and negative European representations of the Other were discouraged and the colonisers, anxious to develop profitable exchange networks, ensured that they studied and understood the economic and social relations of those they met in the colonial situation, often to the point of adopting their conventions (see Trigger 1985: 195, 224-5, 298, 341-2). Additionally, colonisation was often initiated with the intention of incorporating the indigenous population into the 'civilisation' that the colonisers thought that they were creating. In the case of Australia, it was initially expected that the Aboriginal population would be a source of manual labour, and it was only when Aborigines resisted this that a different strategy of subordination and genocide was subsequently effected, with representations of the Other being reconstructed accordingly (Miles 1987a: 107, 189-91).

Second, colonisation was not without its political and ideological repercussions within the emergent European nation states. Both the principle and the particular practices of colonisation evinced political opposition, in the course of which contrary representations of the colonised Other were produced. Images of colonised populations therefore became the object of conflict, in the course of which the content of competing (although often overlapping) representations shifted. For example, from the late eighteenth century, both the use of enslaved African labour in the Caribbean and North America and the slave trade became the focus of a major campaign of opposition within Britain (see Bolt 1969, Temperley 1972, Anstey 1975, Davis 1984). This gave rise to a wide-ranging debate about the nature and capacities of African populations, in the course of which distinct representations of the African *qua* Other were articulated (for example, Davis 1984: 225-6), including abolitionist representations which implied that the African had the capacity to adopt Christianity and British marriage practices (Walvin 1986: 151-2), although the consequences of abolition were subsequently to be interpreted in largely negative terms (Walvin 1986: 84).

Given the temporal length and spatial extent of colonisation, in combination with these factors, it is impossible to offer a comprehensive analysis of the representation of the colonised Other here. There are reasons to focus briefly on British representations of African populations (for representations of other colonised populations, see, for example, Kiernan 1972, Bearce 1982). First, Africa was involved in many different phases of British colonialism over a period of four hundred years and therefore representations of the African populations constitute a central pillar of the British colonial heritage. Second, representations of the African as Other become increasingly interwoven with justifications for, as well as opposition to, the enslavement of the African in the Americas. This has led to the formulation of over-deterministic assertions to the effect that economic interests required a theory of inherent inferiority in order to justify African slavery (for example, Fryer 1984: 134), a functionalist assertion which raises important theoretical questions.

When evaluated in the light of the historical evidence, such claims are difficult to sustain in their rigorous form, not least because they fail to explain the development of earlier representations of Africans. Thus it is not that functionalist accounts are mistaken in any absolute way, but rather that they are incomplete by virtue of their simplistic, non-dialectical nature. Nevertheless, despite this specific focus upon representations of Africans, it should be noted that representations of other colonial Others exhibit both continuity and discontinuity with the former. For example, one striking continuity in British representations of the colonised Other is the attribution of excessive and unrestrained sexuality to a number of different colonised populations (for example, Kiernan 1972: 59, 255-60).

We have already seen that from the time of the earliest contacts between Europeans and Africans, European discourse noted African skin colour and nakedness in order to signify difference. It also noted that Africans were not Christian believers, and as a result they were represented as 'heathens' (see Jordan 1968: 20-1). Thus, this European discourse reflected back what the African was not in order to affirm difference and employed both phenotypical and cultural criteria: the African was defined as simultaneously physically and culturally different (Curtin, 1965: 30). A number of additional characteristics were attributed to the African during the seventeenth and eighteenth centuries and after, in the course of which the African was known to Europeans, and particularly the British, as a slave, both in the colonies and within Britain (Fryer 1984: 155, Walvin 1986: 80-2).

First, the African was represented as exhibiting a potent sexuality. African women were considered to be especially desirous of sexual intercourse while African men were thought to possess an unusally large penis and to be particularly virile and lusty (Jordan 1968: 151, 158-9, Fryer 1984: 140, 159). Second, in the light of the earlier representations of wildness and monstrosity, the African was attributed with a bestial character and there was much speculation about the origin and consequences of the supposed physical similarities between Africans and apes, both of which were 'discovered' by Europeans at the same time in a common geographical location. Indeed, some Europeans suggested that sexual intercourse occurred between Africans and apes (Jordan 1968: 28-32, 238, Fryer 1984: 138). Third, the African was represented as possessing a specific character consisting of both positive and negative attributes. On the one hand, s/he was considered to be lazy, superstitious, ferocious, and a coward, and on the other to be polite, noble, and respectful of the elderly (Curtin 1965: 222-4, Barker 1978: 104). Fourth, the early charge of cannibalism was elaborated throughout the period under examination (Barker 1978: 129).

This emphasis upon physical and animalistic characteristics (but in combination with certain cultural attributes) was used to advance a conception of the African as living in a condition of savagery, a definition which placed the African far below the European on the European scale of human progress (Curtin 1965: 63-5, Walvin 1986: 77). In other words, the African was less civilised, a barbarian, by virtue of supposedly looking more like a beast and behaving in ways that approximated to the behaviour of beasts (Jordan 1968: 24-5, 97). Although for a majority of European opinion, this condition of barbarity and savagery was negatively evaluated, it was regarded by a significant minority, particularly during the eighteenth century, as expressive of a moral superiority because the African was thought to live a life that was more natural as a result of being closer to nature (Curtin 1965: 48-51, Fryer 1984: 145). Here we find the reproduction of the discourse of the noble savage.

There is no doubt that, in European eyes, the African was different. But was the difference sufficient to warrant designation as being non-human? And how was the difference explained? Concerning the former, prior to the late eighteenth century, it was rarely claimed that the African was less than human. Although the African was considered to be bestial and savage, European discourse also noted the existence of other characteristics that denoted a common status as a human being, including language (Curtin 1965: 35, Barker 1978: 47-50). This was buttressed by the centrality of Christianity, and specifically the Biblical explanation for the creation of humanity and the human presence on earth, to European thought (Barker 1978: 88). Throughout the eighteenth century the idea of the Great Chain of Being (Lovejoy 1936), the essence of the idea being that God had created all living things and had organised them into a hierarchy of existence, was used to order the natural and social world. Human beings were higher in this hierarchy than animals, and Africans (similarly created by God as human beings) shared this position with Europeans. But the centrality of the idea of hierarchy to the Great Chain of Being permitted the ranking of the different groups of human beings identified by European thought. Consequently, the African was both different and lower on the scale relative to the European.

For most of the seventeenth and eighteenth centuries, the predominant explanation for the existence of the African as a different sort of human being drew upon environmentalist arguments (Barker 1978: 79) which had a long history. The physical appearance of the African, and specifically the colour of the African's skin, increased in significance as a sign of differentiation (Jordan 1968: 216-17, 512), as therefore did the debate about its origin and purpose. The Christian belief in common origin implied that the African's skin colour had been acquired after God's creation of the human species, but by the late eighteenth century the claim that blackness was the result of God's curse was no longer considered satisfactory and the argument that climate was the key determinant increased in significance (Jordan 1968: 525). Specifically it was argued that the heat of the sun in tropical regions either burnt the skin, or caused it to change colour as protection against the heat. Additionally, some argued that once this transformation had occurred, blackness became an inherited characteristic (Curtin 1965: 40-1, Jordan 1968: 11, Barker 1978: 85).

Climate was believed to determine not only phenotypical features of the African but also cultural characteristics. For example, the attributed quality of laziness was also explained by reference to the heat of the sun. But climate was not considered to be the sole environmental determinant. Samuel Stanhope Smith, an American academic, published an essay in 1787 in which he argued that the human species had originated in Asia in a 'civilised' form and that subsequent migrations were followed by a 'degeneration' into the condition of savagery and by gradual alterations in physical appearance. The causes of these transformations were identified as climate, the state of society and habits of living. Smith placed considerable emphasis upon the latter two factors and this environmentalist argument continued to predominate in American and European discourse in the late eighteenth century (Jordan 1968: 487, 513-15, also Popkin 1974: 139, Barker 1978: 52, 79).

Environmentalist arguments implied that the characteristics attributed to the African were, in principle, subject to modification. If it was argued that the African was a savage, it could also be argued that it was a human condition that could be improved (Barker 1978: 99, also Curtin 1965: 66). Hence Stanhope Smith, for example, claimed that Africans in America were becoming more capable of instruction and that their physical appearance was undergoing modification (Jordan 1968: 515-16). Environmentalism therefore sustained strategies for the 'civilisation' of the African: heathenness and savagery were the consequences of circumstances that could be changed by interventions such as missionary work and plantation production (for example, Curtin 1965: 123-39, 259-86). The idea of the 'civilising mission' was of particular significance during the nineteenth century colonial expansion of Europe, especially into Africa (Kiernan 1972: 24).

This dominant discourse about African characteristics and their determinants had implications for the economic role that many Africans were forced to perform in the Americas. The acquisition and exploitation of African labour power under conditions of slavery was justified, first, by the claim that Africans were specifically suited to work under tropical conditions, unlike Europeans (Curtin 1961: 104, 1965: 116, Barker 1978: 61). The logic of environmentalism implied that this suitability could be acquired, although this seemed to be less readily accepted by Europeans concerning themselves, implying a degree of ambiguity concerning the consistency of environmentalism as an explanation for the hypothesised differences between Europeans and Africans. This ambiguity was partially removed in the nineteenth century with the emergence of the discourse of 'race'. Second, it was justified by the argument that the provision of labour power offered the African an opportunity to escape from the condition of savagery. Entry into slave relations of production therefore permitted Africans to take a step down the road of 'progress' towards 'civilisation', placing them in the first instance in an economic position similar to that of the European poor (Kiernan 1972: 242, Barker 1978: 68, 151-2, 160, 198, also chapter 4).

In sum, certainly up to the end of the eighteenth century, the predominant European representations of the African explicitly or implicitly conceded that the differences exhibited by the latter were not inherent in the sense of fixed and inevitable. Consequently, the incorporation of the African in slave relations of production was not widely legitimated by an argument which alleged that the African was biologically suited to slavery. Such arguments were being advanced by the late eighteenth century, but they had only a minority status (Barker 1978: 52, but see Walvin 1986: 73-9). However, although the predominant view was that the African was a human being, part of God's creation, and exhibited characteristics subject to environmental influence, the African was nevertheless defined as an inferior human being. The representation of the African as Other signified phenotypical and cultural characteristics as evidence of this inferiority and the attributed condition of Africans therefore constituted a measure of European progress and civilisation. The sense of Otherness was increasingly, although not exclusively, grounded in skin colour (Curtin 1965: 39, Jordan 1968: 7), and sustained by the attribution of a number of other negatively evaluated characteristics.

THE SIGNIFICANCE OF SCIENCE

There is widespread agreement amongst historians that a major transformation occurred in European representations of the Other as a result of the secularisation of culture and the growth, and increasing hegemony, of science. These developments interacted with the emergence of the idea of 'race' in European thought, an idea that was taken up by scientific enquiry and increasingly attributed with a narrow and precise meaning, beginning in the late eighteenth century. As a result, the sense of difference embodied in European representations of the Other became interpreted as a difference of 'race', that is, as a primarily *biological* and *natural* difference which was inherent and unalterable. Moreover, the supposed difference was presented as scientific (that is, objective) fact. This discourse of 'race', although the product of 'scientific' activity, came to be widely reproduced throughout Europe, North America and the European colonies in the nineteenth century, becoming, *inter alia*, a component part of common-sense discourse at all levels of the class structure and a basic component of imperialist ideologies (for example, Biddiss 1979b, MacKenzie 1984).

The periodisation of this transformation is, however, more controversial. For example, Fryer argues that this pseudo-scientific ideology emerged orally in the seventeenth century and crystallised in a written form during the eighteenth century (1984: 134). In so arguing, he places much emphasis upon the writing of Edward Long, whose *History of Jamaica* was published in 1774. The argument of the book, according to Barker, was against the dominant view of the time, for the idea of 'race' as proposed by Long was rarely used during the slave trade era (Barker 1978: 42, 52, 164). Jordan has argued that the environmentalist explanation of the Other was becoming less popular only by the first decade of the nineteenth century (1968: 532) while Curtin has claimed that the idea of 'race', and its legitimation by science, did not predominate before 1840 (1965: 29). For our purposes, the fact of the transformation is more important than the precise time at which it occurred.

The idea of 'race' emerged in the English language in the early sixteenth century (Banton 1987: 1) and was used initially largely to explicate European history and nation formation. As it appeared in historical writing, the idea of 'race' referred to those various groups which, collectively, constituted the populations of emergent nation states such as England and France, and which supposedly exhibited qualities which were subsequently transformed into national symbols. The discourse of 'race' therefore played a central role in the creation of myths of national origin (Barzun 1938: 28-50, Poliakov 1974: 1-8), the significance of which will be explored in chapter 3. For example, in the English case, the Anglo-Saxons were defined as a 'race' of people who, from a very early date, formed a significant part of the English population but whose political superiority was diminished by the Norman conquest in 1066. The events of the English civil war in the mid-seventeenth century could then be interpreted as the struggle by the Anglo-Saxon 'race' to reassert their traditions of liberty and democracy against the domination of a Norman monarchy (Poliakov 1974: 37-53, Horsman 1981: 9-24, MacDougall, 1982).

In this usage, 'race' meant lineage or common descent, and identified a population with a common origin and history, but not a population with a fixed biological character (Banton 1977: 16-17, also 1980: 24-7, 1987: 1-27, Guillaumin 1980: 46).

The idea of 'race' took on a new meaning with the development of science and its application to the natural world and, subsequently and more narrowly, to the social world from the late eighteenth century (Banton 1987: 28-64). From this time, 'race' increasingly came to refer to a biological type of human being, and science purported to demonstrate not only the number and characteristics of each 'race', but also a hierarchical relationship between them. Thus it was claimed that all human beings, and therefore every single individual, either belonged to a 'race' or was a product of several 'races', and therefore exhibited the characteristics of that 'race' or those 'races'. Moreover, science purported to demonstrate that the biological characteristics of each 'race' determined a range of psychological and social capacities of each group, by which they could be ranked.

Thus, stated in its most extreme form, 'race' determined economic and cultural characteristics and development (cf. Barzun 1938: 19-21, Banton 1977: 47). This was a discourse of 'race' that may be described as an instance of biological determinism (cf. Gould 1984: 20, Rose *et al*. 1984: 3-15). Thereby, the Other was represented as a biologically distinct entity, as a 'race' apart, whose capacities and achievements were fixed by natural and unalterable conditions which were common to that collectivity. There is now a considerable literature on the ideological career of the idea of 'race' (such as Gossett, 1965, Banton 1977, 1987, Stepan, 1982) and here I draw attention only to those aspects relevant to this general survey of representations of the Other and to the subsequent argument.

First, the scientific assertion of the existence of different biologically-constituted 'races' led eventually to a clash with religious epistemology and religious discourse about the nature and development of the world and the human species. As we have seen, Biblical interpretation suggested that the human species was a divine creation and that all human beings, past and present, were descended from Adam and Eve, implying some ultimate homogeneity of the human species. One method of resolving this problem without questioning the legitimacy of Biblical explanation was to claim that God had responded to the commission of human sin by damnation, and that the descendants of those damned were marked by distinctive features (such as a black skin). Another, with an equally long pedigree, placed less emphasis on divine intervention, maintaining that environmental factors (such as the influence of the sun) had modified the original and single biological form represented by Adam and Eve, creating a number of different types which had subsequently become permanently established by hereditary means. Using this latter argument, many 'race' scientists of the eighteenth and nineteenth centuries were able to claim that their explanation for 'race' differentiation was consistent with Christian theology.

But in the late eighteenth century, scientific analysis revived an objection which had been articulated in the late sixteenth century in Hakluyt's collection of travel writings (see Sanders 1978: 223-4). The counter-claim was that the phenotypical features designated as evidence for the existence of 'race' did not change when members of 'races' moved to different geographical locations and were subjected to different environmental conditions. The case of Africans forcibly moved to, and enslaved within, the United States was often cited to support this view, as was the experience of Europeans resident in the tropical colonies. Both instances were interpreted in such a way as to conclude that the environmental factors, including climate, were incapable of altering the physical features of 'race'. The implication was that distinct 'races' of human beings had always existed and that the hierarchy of inferiority and superiority was therefore natural, inevitable and unalterable. This assault on environmentalism led to a more fundamental conflict with Christian theology (Stanton 1960: 69, 169, Haller 1971: 69-79, Stepan 1982: 36-46). The conclusions to which it gave rise were accorded even greater legitimacy as science occupied an increasingly ascendant position over theology. By the middle of the nineteenth century this theory of polygenism was dominant, and many of its key assumptions survived into the post-Darwinian era (Stocking 1968: 39, 45-6, 55).

Second, the scientific discourse of 'race' did not replace earlier conceptions of the Other. Ideas of savagery, barbarism, and civilisation both predetermined the space that the idea of 'race' occupied but were then themselves reconstituted by it. Thus, as I have demonstrated elsewhere (Miles 1982: 111-12), extant imagery was refracted through the representational prism of 'race', with the result that environmentalism as an explanation for the sense of difference declined in importance. For example, the idea of civilisation emerged in the later part of the eighteenth century. It was a capacity or achievement that was initially considered to be attainable by all human beings, including those thought to be the most savage peoples, given sufficient time and assistance. This implied a plasticity of human characteristics which was challenged in the later nineteenth century by the scientific idea that the human species was divided into permanent and discrete biological groups. As a result, savagery became a fixed condition of the 'Negro' or African 'race', a product of a small brain, and civilisation became an attribute of large-brained 'white' people (Stocking 1968: 35-7, 121-2).

Third, the generation and reproduction of the idea of 'race' was a European and North American phenomenon (for example, Gossett 1965). Many scientific writers contributed, and they drew upon and criticised each other's work, seeking new methods of measurement and solutions to emergent anomalies. The writings of the British theorists, Lord Kames and Charles White, were critically reviewed in the United States by Samuel Stanhope Smith in a book, *Essay on the Causes of the Variety of Complexion and Figure in the Human Species*, published in 1787 (Fredrickson 1972: 72). The science of phrenology originated in the work of Franz Joseph Gall and Johan Gaspar Spurzheim in Germany and was developed by George Combe in Scotland (Gossett 1965: 71-2). In turn, George Combe was a friend of Samuel George Morton, an American who published *Crania Americana* in 1839 and *Crania Aegyptiaca* in 1844 (Gould 1984: 50-69). The cephalic index (a measurement of skulls which involved dividing the length of the skull by the breadth) was invented by Anders Retzius in Sweden (Gossett 1965: 76) and was a stimulus to a significant proportion of the work (much of which was critical) of Paul Broca in Paris (Gould 1984: 98-100).

F. Tiedeman, a German anatomist, measured brains in order to establish differences between 'races', his results stimulating a critical reply from Josiah Clark Nott in the United States (Gossett 1965: 77). Louis Agassiz was a Swiss naturalist who was influenced by Georges Cuvier (himself a French anatomist) and who migrated to the United States in 1846 where he collaborated with Josiah Nott and George Gliddon (Stanton 1960). These two had a major impact on 'race' theory with their book *Types of Mankind*, first published in 1854, which appeared in at least nine editions before the end of the century (Gossett 1965: 65, Banton 1977: 50-2). Thus the increasingly international character of the scientific enterprise was demonstrated by, and facilitated the formulation of, the discourse of 'race'. The consequences were that, as a form of human classification, the scientific idea of 'race' had a widespread circulation, and that all its proponents represented various Others (Africans, North American Indians, Indians) as instances of different and inferior 'races'.

Fourth, although the interrelated ideas of biological type and hierarchy remained a constant feature of the discourse of 'race', the forms of classification and the content of attribution and determination changed over time. For most of the late eighteenth and early nineteenth centuries, 'race' classifications were based upon the phenotypical characteristics of skin colour, hair type, and nose shape, but there was an increasing emphasis upon the dimensions of the skull (Benedict 1983: 22). The latter figured prominently in investigations from the early nineteenth century (Curtin 1965: 366), and considerable effort was expended in assessing, for example, cranial capacity, facial angle and cranial index. Indeed, there was much debate about the relative validity of these different measures. The science of 'race' therefore underwent a complex evolution. In part, this complexity was a function of the essential error of the idea. As each attempt at classification broke down under the weight of logical inconsistency and empirical evidence, a new classification was formulated. But it was also a function of increasing sophistication of measurement (Stocking 1968: 57).

For example, in Germany in the late eighteenth century, Peter Camper claimed to distinguish between 'races' by facial angle, the angle that a line drawn from the chin to the top of the forehead forms with a horizontal line at the base of the chin. He drew the most extreme contrast between 'Greeks' and 'Negroes' (Gossett 1965: 69-70). Somewhat different arguments, but leading to the same conclusion, were advanced by phrenology, the science of the mind, the central claim of which was that the brain was divided into a number of sections, each of which was the basis of a different faculty. It was argued that each 'race' was distinguished by a distinct variation in size and interrelation of these different sections, and not by the weight of the brain or capacity of the skull (Stepan 1982: 21-8). Combe claimed, for example,

> The HINDOOS are remarkable for want of force of character ... Power of mental manifestation bears a proportion to the size of the central organs, and the Hindoo head is small, and the European large, in precise conformity with the different mental characters ... The Hindoo brain indicates a manifest deficiency in the organs of Combativeness and Destructiveness; while, in the European, these parts are amply developed. The Hindoo is cunning, timid and proud; and in him Secretiveness, Cautiousness and Self-Esteem are large in proportion to the organs last mentioned. (Combe 1830: 605-6)

As Fryer expressed it succinctly, on this basis 'phrenology justified empire-building' (1984: 171).

Samuel Morton measured differences between 'races' by filling skulls with mustard seed or lead shot, from which he derived a measure of cranial capacity. He claimed to demonstrate significant differences in cranial capacity between five different 'races' (Caucasian, Mongolian, Malay, American, and Ethiopian) although in his final conclusions, these 'races' were further subdivided into 'families' (see Gould 1984: 54-5). Morton's craniometry was a major influence upon Nott and Gliddon (see Stanton 1960, Gould 1984: 30-72) who assumed that there was a correlation between increasing cranial capacity and a higher level of innate intelligence. Louis Gratiolet offered evidence that the coronal suture of the skull closes, thereby arresting the growth of the brain, at different times for different 'races'. He concluded that this closure occurred earlier amongst 'Negroes' than amongst 'Whites' (Gossett 1965: 75, Gould 1984: 98). The problems are most evident in the increasing complexity of the measurement systems evolved by Paul Broca in his attempt to identify a phenotypical feature that would systematically and consistently demonstrate the existence of a hierarchy of 'races' (Gossett 1965: 76, Gould 1984: 82-107).

Fifth, the scientific notion of 'race' had a universal application. Not only did those who formulated the idea consider themselves to be members of a 'race' but they also identified a hierarchy of 'races' within Europe. Efforts were made in the late nineteenth century, for example, to identify the different 'races' of which the British population was composed, using hair and eye colour and skull measurements (Beddoe 1885). Concerning Europe as a whole, various classifications were devised, the most common being a distinction between Teutonic (or Nordic), Mediterranean, and Alpine 'races' (Ripley 1900: 103-30). In the USA, this classification was combined with an argument that human intelligence was a fixed and hereditary characteristic in order, as we shall see below, to produce a hierarchy of acceptable and unacceptable immigrants (Kamin 1977: 30-51, Gould 1984: 146-233).

Within Europe, representations of the Other as an inferior 'race' focused, amongst others, on the Irish (Curtis 1968, 1971) and Jews (Mosse 1978). This was sustained partly by claiming a biological superiority for the Nordic 'race'. In Germany, Günther (1970) interpreted European history in a book titled *The Racial Elements of European History* (first published in 1927) using the scientific idea of 'race' to refer to human groups with distinct and measurable physical and mental characteristics. He identified the Nordic 'race' as especially creative, with a need for conquest, a special aptitude for military science and a low crime rate, and he feared social decay in Europe as a result of 'the running dry of the blood of the ... Nordic race' (1970: 198). Portentously, he stated that 'the question put to us is whether we have courage enough to make ready for future generations a world cleansing itself racially and eugenically' (1970: 267). Günther was only one of a large number of German (and other European) scholars (and political activists) who employed the scientific discourse of 'race' to assert simultaneously the superiority of the Nordic 'race' and the inferiority of Jews (Mosse 1978: 77-93, 113-27).

Sixth, the scientific conception of 'race' has now been shown to be mistaken, although a number of scientists continue to this day to assert the key ideas in various forms. The exposure of the error had a long genesis which began with the work of Charles Darwin and finished with the emergence of population genetics. The first important step was the formulation of the theory of evolution which questioned in principle the validity of the idea of fixed and permanent biological species. However, when the human species was located in evolutionary theory in Europe in the latter half of the nineteenth century, the idea of 'race' was retained, the argument being that each 'race' could be ranked on an evolutionary scale. Thus, what came to be known as Social Darwinism (Jones 1980, Clark 1984, 1988) asserted that there was a struggle for survival amongst the different human 'races', in the course of which those with lesser intelligence or capacity for 'civilisation' would eventually disappear, their elimination being evidence of their natural inability to evolve. Thus, rather than leading to the rejection of the idea of discrete biological 'races', evolutionary theory was developed initially in a way which endorsed this conception, and the classifiers of the human species (notably the physical anthropologists) continued to produce their typologies (Haller 1971: 121-52, Banton 1977: 89-100, Stepan 1982: 47-110).

A further decisive development was the articulation of the statistical limitations of phenotypical measurement by those who continued to defend the utility of such measurement. The work of Boas in the early twentieth century is particularly important because he also demonstrated the influence of the social environment on physiological features by use of the cephalic index (for example, 1940: 60-75). Boas, then, asserted the existence of biological 'races' but rejected the argument that they were fixed, because of evidence that phenotypical features such as head form did respond to environmental influences (Stocking 1968: 170-80). He also argued that although the world's population could be divided into a number of 'races' using various phenotypical criteria, each such category contained within it a range of variation that overlapped with the variation of any other category. He said, moreover, 'With regard to many characteristics of this kind, we find that the difference between the averages of different races is insignificant as compared to the range of variability that occurs within each race' (Boas 1940: 42). It follows from this that although it may be the case that two populations can be shown to have a different average height, it does not follow that any two individuals selected from these two populations will demonstrate the same difference. In other words, groups differences do not correspond to individual differences (cf. Stocking 1968: 192-3).

The full implications of Darwin's evolutionary theory could only be explored with the emergence of the science of genetics which identified the biological basis of evolutionary processes. Genetics shifted attention partly away from phenotypical differences such as skin colour and analysed biological features which were not evident to the naked eye and which, in a complex interaction with the environment, determined biological changes in the human species. It was generally concluded after the Second World War that the scientific conception of 'race' grounded in the idea of fixed typologies and based upon certain phenotypical features such as skin colour and skull shape does not have any significant scientific meaning or utility. Moreover, it was concluded that there is no causal relationship between physical or genetic characteristics and cultural characteristics. In a phrase, genetics demonstrated that 'race', as defined by scientists from the late eighteenth century, had no scientifically verifiable referent (Boyd 1950, Montagu 1964, 1972).

This has not, however, prevented the continuing use of the term in scientific and everyday language. Concerning the scientific community, some physical anthropologists have continued to assert a 'race' classification using phenotypical features in spite of the genetic and other contrary evidence (for example, Hooton 1947) and the famous UNESCO statements on the nature of 'race' gave some varying, but heavily qualified, approval to this approach (see Montagu 1972: 9, 142, 150). On the other hand, many geneticists have argued that populations can be better distinguished from each other by identifying different frequencies of variable genes, although they acknowledge that the point at which it is decided to distinguish between populations is determined arbitrarily (Boyd 1950: 202-7, Bodmer 1972: 90). They argue that these populations, distinguished not by phenotypical features but by genetic frequencies, should be labelled 'races'. In the light of these different conceptions, and of the claims by other scientists that the 'race' idea has no scientific value at all, it is difficult to identify any utility in continuing to use the term scientifically (cf. Montagu 1972: 63, Jones 1981, see Miles 1982: 18-19).

Concerning the latter, in many different contexts, people have continued to identify the Other by reference to phenotypical features (especially skin colour) which therefore serve as indicative of a significant difference. Moreover, they have continued to use the idea of 'race' to label that difference. As a result, certain sorts of social relations are defined as 'race relations', as social relations between people of different 'races'. Indeed, states legislate to regulate 'race relations', with the result that the reality of 'race' is apparently legitimated in law (Guillaumin 1980). Thus the idea of 'race' has continued to be used in common-sense discourse to identify the Other in many societies, but largely without the sanction of science.

CONCLUSION

The discussion of discourse and representation in this chapter has been detached to a large extent (although not completely) from its political and economic context; consequently, the nature, determinants and consequences of European and North American representations of the Other have not been discussed explicitly. The intention, and result, has been largely descriptive and historical. In order to go on to discuss these matters, it is necessary to summarise the conclusions that should be drawn from the empirical, historical material outlined in this chapter.

First, the process of representing the Other entails a dialectic of representational inclusion and exclusion. By attributing a population with certain characteristics in order to categorise and differentiate it as an Other, those who do so also establish criteria by which they themselves are represented. In the act of defining Africans as 'black' and 'savages', and thereby excluding them from their world, Europeans in the eighteenth and nineteenth centuries were representing themselves as 'white' and 'civilised'. Moreover, by using the discourse of 'race' to exclude and inferiorise, that same discourse, but with inverted meanings, served to include and superiorise: if the population of Africa was represented as a 'race', then the population of Europe is simultaneously represented as a 'race', albeit a supposedly superior one. Hence, the act of representational exclusion is simultaneously an act of inclusion, whether or not Self is explicitly identified in the discourse.

Second, for the European, the Other has not been created exclusively in the colonial context. Representations of the Other have taken as their subject not only the populations of, for example, Africa, the Indian subcontinent, and the Americas but also the populations of different parts of Europe, as well as invasionary and colonising populations, notably from North Africa and the Middle East. Moreover, the Other has been created not only externally to the nation state but also within, most notably in the case of the Jews. Consequently, debate about the nature and origin of representations of the Other cannot be confined to the analysis of European colonialism (although this is not to claim that the colonial experience is of no relevance to understanding the nature and origin of European representations of the Other).

Third, representations of the Other are holistically neither static nor unitary. They have undergone transformation over time, in response to changing circumstances, including the economic and political position of those producing and reproducing the representations. The characteristics attributed to the Other, the evaluation of those characteristics, and the explanations offered for difference, have therefore been altered, although again rarely in a holistic manner. Thus, in the case of the European representation of the African, while skin colour has remained a constant distinguishing feature, representations of savagery and bestiality have been historically variable. Indeed, the evaluative content of European representations has not been consistently negative, and we have seen examples where the qualities identified and attributed have been largely positively evaluated. Moreover, those people who constitute the object of representation, who are created as the Other, also change over time. For example, for a long period of time in European history, the primary Other was found in the Islamic world rather than central and southern Africa.

Hence, when analysing representations of the Other, it is necessary to be alert to the class position of those producing and reproducing them, and to their dynamic and heterogeneous nature, as well as to their more constant features. The analytical implication is that one cannot assume the existence of a simple process of representational reproduction whereby contemporary representations are inherited from the past. Rather, contemporary representations are always the product of historical legacy and active transformation in the light of prevailing circumstances, including the pattern of class relations.

Fourth, for the European, as well as for other populations, somatic features, and particularly skin colour, have been used to represent the Other long before European colonisation. However, exteriorisation by reference to blackness has not consistently correlated with the attribution of additional, negatively evaluated characteristics, and hence the representation of the African within the Greco-Roman world during the third and second centuries BC differs in a number of important respects from that created and reproduced in north west Europe from the seventeenth century. Moreover, representations of the Other have not been based on somatic characteristics alone. Cultural characteristics have also been used, and sometimes to the virtual exclusion of phenotypical features: European representations of the Islamic world extensively utilised images of barbarism and sexuality in the context of a Christian/heathen dichotomy.

Fifth, the development of the discourse of 'race', and its subsequent incorporation into the discourse of science did not entail a complete break with earlier representations of the Other and therefore the creation of completely new means of representational inclusion and exclusion. Within Europe, scientific discourse, and its application to the human species took place in a context of an existing pattern of representation and inferiorisation which it incorporated and theorised by new criteria of secularised validity. Because the emergence of science did not displace these earlier hierarchies of inferiority, including those which used somatic differences to identify the Other, analyses of the representations of the Other which focus exclusively on the career of the discourse of 'race' arbitrarily detach that history from its roots.

This is not to minimise the transformation entailed in the gradual epistemological shift from religion to science as the criterion by which to measure and evaluate the nature of the social and material world. This transformation was highly significant in so far as it permitted and rationalised a method of inquiry which sought to investigate a level of reality which lay below that revealed by immediate and unmediated observation, and to advance explanations which were not confined to references to 'divine will'. Nevertheless, the development of science did not, by itself, guarantee accuracy and veracity, partly because the agenda for scientific investigation was shaped by a variety of additional interests and by a particular pattern of international economic and political relations.

2

Conceptual inflation

INTRODUCTION

Against the background of the selective, historical review of European and North American representations of the Other, I now consider the problem of defining racism. Throughout chapter 1, I referred to discourse about the Other rather than to racism. This was intentional. Some analysts will wish to describe all these above instances as racism while others will want to distinguish different categories of discourse, labelling only some as instances of racism. Thus, if there was some general agreement between these groups of writers that the content of chapter 1 constituted an accurate, if not complete, history of discourses of the Other, their disagreement would result largely from the fact that they used different *concepts* of racism. The previous chapter therefore provides an initial historical contextualisation for the conceptual problem to be considered in this chapter.

In using racism as a concept to describe and explain aspects of the structure and processes of concrete social formations, it is necessary first to know what the word refers to, what particularity it identifies. That this is considered to be problematic may appear surprising in the first instance, given the generally common understanding of, for example, Nazi discourse about the Jews, the justifications for the establishment of apartheid in South Africa, and official legitimations of British colonial settlement and rule. Nevertheless, the concept of racism is contested. In essence, the debate concerns the scope of the concept, and in two senses.

First, for those who define the concept as referring to a particular instance of *ideology*, there is disagreement about the form and content that ideology must possess to warrant categorisation as racism. Second, some writers have claimed that the concept should be used to refer to not only ideology but also intentional practices and/or unintended processes or consequences. There has been, therefore, a process of conceptual inflation whereby the concept has been redefined to refer to a wider range of phenomena. The intention of this chapter is to review critically this process of conceptual inflation while chapter 3 will offer a resolution of some of the problems identified below.

In order to do this, an explanatory comment about the concept of ideology is necessary. The meaning of this concept is also widely contested (for an overview, see Larrain 1979, 1983, Sayer 1979, Billig 1982, Macdonnell 1986) but in this chapter it is used generally to refer to any discourse which, as a whole (but not necessarily in terms of all of its component parts) represents human beings, and the social relations between human beings, in a distorted and misleading manner. Thus, ideology is a specific form of discourse. The discourse need not be systematic or logically coherent, nor be intentionally created and reproduced in order to deceive or mislead, even though that is its consequence. Such a concept presumes an alternative epistemological position, from the occupancy of which it is possible to demonstrate the falsity of the discourse defined as ideology, a position that is identified below as science.

RACISM AS IDEOLOGY

Although the word 'racism' is now widely used in common-sense, political, and academic discourse, it is of very recent origin (cf. Leech 1986). There is no reference to the word in the *Oxford English Dictionary* (*OED*) of 1910 (although there are entries for race and racial). The *OED Supplement* of 1982 defines racism as 'the theory that distinctive human characteristics and abilities are determined by race' and records its first appearance in the English language in the 1930s. Critics of scientific theories of 'race' prior to this decade did not use a concept of racism to identify their ideological object. For example, in a wide-ranging critique published in the late 1920s, Friedrich Hertz referred to 'race hatred' (1928: 1-19). The term racism was used as a title for a book written by Magnus Hirschfeld in 1933-4 in German and subsequently translated into English and published in Britain in 1938. In *Racism*, Hirschfeld set out to refute those arguments of the nineteenth century which, as I have shown in the previous chapter, claimed the mantle of science to sustain the notion of the existence of discrete 'races', hierarchically ordered. But he does so without offering any formal definition of racism and without clarifying how racism is to be distinguished from the concept of xenophobia, which he also employs in his argument (1938: 227).

The original definition and use of the word arose from the coincidence of two processes. The first was, as I have outlined in chapter 1, the growing body of scientific evidence which undermined the idea of 'races' as natural, discrete and fixed subdivisions of the human species, each with its distinct and variable cultural characteristics and capacity for 'civilisation'. The second was the reaction to the rise of Fascism in Germany and the use of the 'race' idea, legitimated partly by reference to science, by Hitler and the German Nazi party in their identification of Jews as an alien and inferior 'race' in Germany (Maser 1970). As the Nazi campaign against the Jews in Germany unfolded (see Krausnick *et al.* 1968, Peukert, 1987), there developed elsewhere in Europe and North America an increasing awareness of the way in which the discourse of 'race' was being used to legitimate the exclusion and genocide of the Jews and other sections of the German population. It became an imperative for some academics and scientists, as well as political activists, to formulate a coherent rejection of the way in which the 'race' idea was utilised in Nazi Germany.

These two developments reinforced each other. There was an intensification of the debate about the scientific status of the discourse of 'race', evident in the publication during the 1930s and 1940s of a number of books which were explicitly critical of either a certain usage of the idea or, in certain instances, the idea itself. Although there was no unanimity amongst these critics, the fact that a critical appraisal of the claim that 'race' was a biological fact was taking place was indicative of a paradigm change within the academic, scientific world. The object of that critical appraisal came to be defined as racism (for example, Hirschfeld 1938).

The absence of unanimity can be demonstrated by a brief review of the key literature of the period. In *We Europeans: A Survey of 'Racial' Problems*, Huxley and Haddon (1935) argued that there was no scientific evidence to sustain the idea of distinct and discrete 'races' and that 'racial biology' was a pseudo-science. Much of the book consisted of a scientific refutation of classifications based on somatic characteristics and an evaluation of the contribution of genetics to an understanding of human variation, from which Huxley and Haddon concluded that the word 'race' should be dropped from scientific vocabulary, to be replaced by 'ethnic group' (1935: 108, 164, 268). Their justification for this recommendation was, at least in part, political.

They argued that the term 'race', like many other pseudo-scientific terms, could be used to 'rationalise emotion' (1935: 262) and that science had a responsibility to identify the truth value of ideas employed in political life (Huxley and Haddon 1935: 287). They made reference to the then contemporary situation in Germany, specifically denying that Nordic or Jewish 'races' existed and identified Nazi theories of 'race' as a 'creed of passionate racialism' (1935: 277). They continued, 'Racialism is a myth, and a dangerous myth at that. It is a cloak for selfish economic aims which in their uncloaked nakedness would look ugly enough' (1935: 287). This myth of racialism was explained as an attempt to justify nationalism.

While Haddon and Huxley rejected any scientific use of the idea of 'race' and, almost as an afterthought, employed the concept of racialism to refer to Nazi ideologies of 'race', their text demonstrates a contradiction over the significance of biological classification. Although they argued that 'any biological arrangement of the types of European man [*sic*] is still largely a subjective process' (1935: 166), they proceeded to construct one using 'those characters which are the most convenient and readily observed' (1935: 169), specifically skin colour, and hair and nose type. They concluded

> We can thus distinguish three major groupings of mankind:
> (1) Black woolly hair, dark brown or black skin, and a broad nose.
> (2) Wavy or curly hair of any colour from black to flaxen, dark brown to white skin, and a typically medium or narrow nose with usually a high bridge.
> (3) Straight lank dark hair, yellowish skin, nose with a tendency to be broad and low-bridged. (1935: 169-70)

Despite their mastery of the scientific evidence, from which they concluded that biological classifications were subjective, they nevertheless reproduced a taxonomy that differed only from nineteenth century classifications in that it did not label these groups as 'Negroid', 'Caucasian' and 'Mongoloid' and described them as 'ethnic groups' rather than 'races'.

Jacques Barzun was more consistent in his pursuit of an objective similar to that of Huxley and Haddon. In *Race, A Study in Modern Superstition* (1938) Barzun offered a critical history of the discourse of 'race' in order to demonstrate that 'race-thinking is ... a form of erroneous thinking that can be charged with a dozen ulterior motives' (1938: 26) but he did not devise any form of biological taxonomy of the human species. He too made specific reference to Nazi Germany, identifying the Third Reich as 'the most blatant apostle of racialism' (1938: 6), but focusing more broadly on 'racialism as a European phenomenon' (1938: 10). Although Barzun was not explicit, he (like Huxley and Haddon) seemed to use the concept of racialism rather than racism to identify what he referred to as 'race thinking'.

A rather different argument was offered in a book first published in 1942. In *Race and Racism*, Ruth Benedict rejected Barzun's claim that race is a modern superstition, asserting that 'race is a classification based on traits which are hereditary' (1983: 6) and that race constitutes a 'scientific field of enquiry' (1983: 96). Benedict legitimated much of the nineteenth century anthropological and biological classification reviewed in the previous chapter when she asserted that three main races can be identified, the Caucasian, Mongoloid, and Negroid (1983: 31-2). But she distinguished what she defined as the scientific study of race from racism which she identified as, 'the dogma that one ethnic group is condemned by nature to congenital inferiority and another group is destined to congenital superiority' (1983: 97). Therefore, the concept of racism refers to a set of claims which are contrary to the scientific evidence and which therefore constitute a denial of science. Additionally, she claimed that racism is a temporally and geographically specific phenomenon when she argued that 'racism is a creation of our own time', of 'high European civilisation' (1983: 2, cf. Puzzo 1964, Montagu 1974: 21-2).

In the same year that *Race and Racism* was first published, Ashley Montagu's text *Man's* [sic] *Most Dangerous Myth: The Fallacy of Race* appeared. In it, Montagu defined racism as an ideology which

> alleged that something called 'race' is the prime determiner of all the important traits of body and soul, of character and personality, of human beings and nations. And it is further alleged that this something called 'race' is a fixed and unchangeable part of the germ plasm, which, transmitted from generation to generation, unfolds in each people as a typical expression of personality and culture. (Montagu 1974: 14)

Despite an agreement on the definition of the concept of racism, Montagu's use of quotation marks signals his disagreement with Benedict's claim that 'race' is a biological reality which can be studied scientifically. He argued (1974: 62; also 1964: 18), 'Based as it is on unexamined facts and unjustifiable generalisations, it were better that the term "race", being so weighed down with false meaning, be dropped altogether from the vocabulary.'

Two analytical points arise from this literature. First, the original concept of racism presupposed the existence of a discourse of 'race' because it was defined to refer to the nineteenth century beliefs that the human species consisted of a number of different 'races', identified phenotypically, and that these 'races' were ranked in a hierarchy of superiority and inferiority. This interlock was evident in the very title of Benedict's book, *Race and Racism* (1983). Second, the act of labelling the 'race-thinking' of the nineteenth century as racism was simultaneously to label it as a scientific error. Within the scientific arena, this challenge to the nineteenth century idea of 'race' led in two directions, one of which retained this interlock while the other broke it. Thus, respectively, the critique led to either a retention of the discourse of 'race' accompanied by a redefinition of the referent or a rejection of both the discourse of 'race' and the reality to which it supposedly referred.

Benedict's argument was therefore rather different from those advanced by Huxley and Haddon, Barzun, and Montagu. While the latter sought to reject the discourse of 'race', Benedict wished to retain it as a scientific concept and she sought to do so by defining as racism that particular usage of the discourse of 'race' as biological hierarchy which could not be justified by science. In this way, Benedict's definition of racism served to sustain and legitimate the discourse of 'race'. Nevertheless, all these writers were agreed on using a concept of racism or racialism to refer to a very specific ideology, that is, to the product of late eighteenth and nineteenth century scientific thought. So if we consider the long history of European representations of the Other outlined in chapter 1, only those advanced from the late eighteenth century which embodied an explicit discourse of 'race' in order to refer to a discrete biological group can be identified as racism. All earlier representations of the Other are excluded from this definition of racism and therefore qualify as instances of some other ideology or ideologies. It has been common to define these earlier representations as 'ethnocentrism' (for example, Puzzo 1964: 579-81, Montagu 1974: 21).

The experience of the Second World War and the knowledge of the consequences of Hitler's 'final solution' to the 'Jewish question' (Dawidowicz 1977, Fleming 1986) led to new initiatives after 1945 to try to prevent the discourse of 'race' from being used for similar political purposes in the future. The most significant was undertaken by UNESCO, and claimed the status of science, and of international collaboration and unanimity, to legitimate its objectives. During the 1950s and 1960s, UNESCO assembled, on four separate occasions, a group of scientists of international reputation who were asked to summarise the scientific evidence concerning the nature of 'race'. The objective was to demonstrate that the barbarism of the 'final solution' rested on 'a scientifically untenable premise' (Montagu 1972: x). Of the four UNESCO statements on 'race', only the fourth explicitly addressed the issue of a definition of racism. The first two statements did not employ the term at all while the third noted that the biological evidence contradicted the 'tenets of racism' (Montagu 1972: 154) without defining what they were. These three statements were intended primarily to demolish 'the myth that race determines mental aptitude, temperament, or social habits' (Montagu 1972: x) and only the fourth broadened its scope in order to address directly the nature of racism.

This fourth UNESCO statement repeats (but, as we shall see shortly, also inflates) the definition offered by Benedict and other writers of the 1930s and 1940s. Thus it defines racism as a falsification of the scientific knowledge about human biology: 'Racism falsely claims that there is a scientific basis for arranging groups hierarchically in terms of psychological and cultural characteristics that are immutable and innate' (Montagu 1972: 158). In common with Benedict, this definition includes those arguments which mistakenly identify a hierarchy of human groups, each of which is in some way naturally and inevitably distinct from all others.

The essence of Benedict's definition was repeated in the 1960s and 1970s by writers such as Van den Berghe (1978: 11) and Banton (1970). The latter defined racism in the late 1960s as 'the doctrine that a man's [sic] behaviour is determined by stable inherited characters deriving from separate racial stocks having distinctive attributes and usually considered to stand to one another in relations of superiority and inferiority' (Banton 1970: 18). He too was referring exclusively to the nineteenth century scientific arguments about 'race', as a result of which, given that those ideas had been discredited by science, he concluded that racism was dead (1970: 28, also Puzzo 1964: 586). Banton subsequently defined this nineteenth century scientific doctrine as 'racial typology' rather than racism (1977: 27-8, 47, 1980: 28) and so, at least to his satisfaction, abolished racism as a concept in sociological analysis (Banton 1987: ix).

Banton's rejection of the concept of racism is indicative of four problems that arose from the fact that this original concept of racism was shaped by the particular historical context, and political strategies, of the 1930s and 1940s. First, the concept of racism was forged largely in the course of a conscious attempt to withdraw the sanction of science from a particular meaning of the idea of 'race'. This required a rejection of the product of nineteenth century science which thereby underwent a transformation from the status of an assumed fact to that of ideology. But in the process of effecting this transformation, racism was defined narrowly to refer exclusively to this specific ideological object, with the result that when it was applied to other social contexts or when the social context changed, the concept proved vacuous. Simply, in the absence of this nineteenth century discourse of 'race', with all of its correlate assertions, the analyst could only conclude that racism did not exist or had evaporated.

This was recognised by those who drafted the fourth UNESCO statement on 'race'. The statement notes that the widespread exposure of the falsity of assertions that the human species is composed of a hierarchy of biologically distinct groups has transformed the content of racism.

> Whenever it [racism] fails in its attempts to prove that the source of group differences lies in the biological field, it falls back upon justifications in terms of divine purpose, cultural differences, disparity of educational standards or some other doctrine which would serve to mask its continued racist beliefs. (Montagu 1972: 159)

In other words, the exposure of nineteenth century racism as a false and politically dangerous doctrine has changed the social context, with the result that explicit assertions that 'race' determines culture either cannot be sustained or are not articulated in the public domain because they are beyond the boundaries of acceptable argument (although they continue to be articulated in the informal domain and have certainly not disappeared). One therefore has the choice of concluding either that racism has disappeared, as

Banton and others have done, or that the definition of racism should be revised in order to express the claim that racism is an ideology that takes a number of different forms.

I shall argue later in favour of this second option (but also against the specific formulation outlined in the UNESCO statement) but for the present purposes I presuppose this argument in order to sustain my case that Benedict's definition of racism, because it is a historically specific product, must have limited applicability outside of that context. Once this is recognised, there is an alternative to Banton's rejection of the concept of racism; this is to refer to this ideological product of nineteenth century science as 'scientific racism'. Comas has used this terminology (1961) and I (Miles 1982: 21), along with others (for example, Rich 1986: 13), have followed and elaborated upon this conceptual strategy. This presumes a generic definition of racism, of which this scientific form is but one instance, a matter to which I also return later in this chapter.

Second, this early definition of racism, by focusing on the product of nineteenth century scientific theorising, tended to presume that racism was always, and therefore was only, a structured and relatively coherent set of assertions, usually sustained by reference to formally organised empirical evidence. This is demonstrated in Banton's early definition of racism as a doctrine. Such a definition excludes less formally structured assertions, stereotypical ascriptions and symbolic representations which draw much of their meaning from unstated assertions or assumptions of causal determination and which in themselves do not meet the criterion of constituting an explicitly 'logical' structure (cf. Rex 1970: 12).

Third, this original definition of the concept of racism tended to remain inextricably entangled with, and consequently to legitimate, the idea of 'race'. Because the definition of racism was confined to the nineteenth century discourse of 'race', in a context where either the idea of 'race' was given scientific legitimacy (as Benedict did) or was not explicitly rejected on the grounds of having no real referent, the concept of racism, while rejecting as unscientific the formulation that 'race' determines culture, left the idea of 'race' unquestioned and unchallenged. Thus, racism was exposed as a false doctrine, but it was conceded, certainly by default, and sometimes explicitly, that nevertheless the human species was divided into 'races'. In Barzun's terms, 'race-thinking' remained, sanctioning some form of biological classification as meaningful and useful.

Fourth, because racism became a label attached to a set of beliefs about 'race' that were used to justify exclusionary actions and, ultimately, genocide, the historical context ensured that the concept of racism carried with it a prominent moral and political content. To refer to a set of assertions as racism, and to the person who articulated them as a racist, consequently associated those ideas and those persons with Hitler and Fascism. Hence, viewed from within a liberal and humanitarian tradition, the ideas and arguments that the concept of racism came to refer to were morally reprehensible and politically unacceptable to those writers who coined and employed the term. Thus, it was a concept that claimed scientific justification for its rejection of the claims of nineteenth century scientific investigation but which also embodied a clear value judgement about what were acceptable beliefs.

My argument to this point is that the historical context in which racism was identified initially as an ideology shaped its definition in such a way that it had little or no meaning outside of that context. As we have seen, the UNESCO statement of 1967 sought to revise this definition on the basis of the reasoning that an ideology need not have a biological referent but may utilise 'justifications in terms of divine purpose, cultural differences, disparity of educational standards or some other doctrine which would serve to mask its continued racist beliefs' (Montagu 1972: 159). In other words, racism cannot be identified exclusively as an ideology with a specific biological content or reference.

One of the members of the UNESCO group of scientific experts who met in 1967 was John Rex who subsequently advanced a very similar argument in the course of critically evaluating Banton's early analysis of the nature of racism. Suggesting that biological arguments which identify and justify group differentiation have functional substitutes derived from quite different discourses, Rex argued that

> the common element in all these theories is that they see the connection between membership of a particular group and of the genetically related sub-groups (i.e. families and lineages) of which that group is compounded and the possession of evaluated qualities as completely deterministic. (Rex 1970: 159)

In other words, the concept of racism refers to any argument which suggests that the human species is composed of discrete groups in order to legitimate inequality between those groups of people.

According to this definition, the concept of racism should refer to the function rather than the content of discourses: the focus of the definition is no longer upon a particular ideological content but the intention and/or consequence of any deterministic assertion about group differences. Using such a definition to analyse the historical material presented in chapter 1 leads to a generally inclusive conclusion. Most, if not all, of the representations of the Other discussed there identified the Other as a member of a distinct group by virtue of possessing a variety of biological and/or cultural characteristics, and most also justified either potentially or actually unequal treatment. For example, European representations of Muslims asserted that they were naturally violent and lascivious, an assertion that qualifies as an instance of racism according to Rex's definition.

But this inflation of the scope of the concept includes the majority, if not all, of the examples cited in chapter 1. By widening the definition to include any deterministic attribution of qualities to a group identified as biologically or culturally distinct in order to justify inequality, it therefore includes arguments such as 'Women should not be put in positions of responsibility because their emotional character prevents them from making rational decisions', and 'I don't go to Italian restaurants because Italians are rude'. It therefore becomes impossible to differentiate arguments which, as in the former example, might otherwise be designated as sexist. Moreover, what has become, at least in part, a functionalist definition of racism must therefore exclude purely descriptive statements when they are not intended to, or when they do not explicitly, justify inequality.

Thus, by focusing on the function of deterministic assertions without considering their content, this revised concept of racism simultaneously broadens and narrows the range of racist ideology to include deterministic arguments about women and populations distinguished by nationality, and to exclude deterministic claims which do not function to justify exclusion (Miles 1982: 72-9). If we wish to retain a concept of racism that refers exclusively to ideology, we therefore have to find a way to revise this inflated concept. But before we consider this, we must evaluate a further expansion of the meaning of the concept.

INSTITUTIONAL RACISM

The 1967 UNESCO statement inflated the concept when it offered a further definition of racism as 'antisocial beliefs and acts which are based on the fallacy that discriminatory intergroup relations are justifiable on biological grounds' (Montagu 1972: 158). While the UNESCO statement neglected to justify and failed to explore the implications of this inflation of the scope of the concept to include practices as well as discourse, other writers have pursued the logic of this inflation in two, interrelated, directions since the late 1960s. The first has been to define as racism all processes which, intentionally or not, result in the continued exclusion of a subordinate group. This is commonly captured by the concept of institutional racism. The second has been to define as racism all those activities and practices which are intended to protect the advantages of a dominant group and/or to maintain or widen the unequal position of a subordinate group. In both instances, the dominant and subordinate groups are usually designated by reference to skin colour, that is, as 'whites' and 'blacks' respectively, the corollary being that racism is, by definition, a process effected, intentionally or otherwise, by 'white' people to the disadvantage of 'black' people.

Above, I have argued that a key historical determinant of the early definition of racism was the rise of Fascism and the Nazi practice of genocide in Europe. These new definitions were shaped by a quite different historical context, the political struggle of Afro-Americans against their position of inequality in the United States. The experience of material deprivation and exclusionary practice in the southern rural areas and in the northern cities of the United States gave rise to political resistance which increased in scope and intensity during the twentieth century (see Essien-Udom 1962, Pinkney 1976, Blair 1977, Sitkoff 1981). In the context of the resistance and riots of the 1960s, Carmichael and Hamilton published *Black Power* (1968) which presented what became an influential political analysis and strategy. They defined racism as 'the predication of decisions and policies on considerations of race for the purpose of *subordinating* a racial group and maintaining control over that group' (1968: 3). They distinguished between overt and individual racism on the one hand and covert and institutional racism (which they also described as colonialism) on the other. The former was defined as explicit actions by individuals and the latter as those actions and inactions which maintain 'black' people in a disadvantaged situation and which rely on 'the active and pervasive operation of anti-black attitudes and practices' (1968: 5). Thus, the concept of racism was expanded in meaning to include not only beliefs but, more important, all actions, individual and institutional, which had the consequence of sustaining or increasing the subordination of 'black' people.

A number of American academics took up this idea of institutional racism and attempted to give it more coherence and a greater analytical power in an academic context where the dominant concept was prejudice and the dominant paradigm was social psychological in nature, a concept and paradigm that located the origin of the problem in the cognitive errors of individuals (Henriques, 1984: 65-81). Not all of these attempts achieved these objectives. Knowles and Prewitt (1969), for example, fail to offer a formal definition of institutional racism but seem to use it to mean practices within institutions which ensure that 'black citizens ... are consistently penalised for reasons of color' but which may be neither intentional nor motivated by 'conscious bigotry' (1969: 4-7). Blauner is more careful to define his concepts explicitly. He argues that the definition of the concept of racism should be extended so as to refer not only to individual prejudiced attitudes but also to processes that sustain 'white' domination:

> The processes that maintain domination - control of whites over non-whites - are built into the major social institutions ... Thus there

is little need for prejudice as a motivating force. Because this is true, the distinction between racism as an objective phenomenon, located in the actual existence of domination and hierarchy, and racism's subjective concomitants of prejudice and other motivations and feelings is a basic one. (Blauner 1972: 9-10)

Thus, Blauner expanded the concept of racism so as to refer to two different phenomena which are very similar to Carmichael and Hamilton's distinction between individual racism and institutional racism. Significantly, Blauner fails to define the criteria by which one might identify either 'prejudice' or those processes which ensure the 'control of whites over non-whites'.

The second direction I have identified is represented by Wellman who also explicitly extends the definition of racism to refer to more than 'prejudiced beliefs'. While Wellman uses the concept to refer to personal prejudice, he argues that 'the essential feature of racism is ... the defense of a system from which advantage is derived on the basis of race' (1977: 221-2) and hence he claims that 'racism is a structural relationship based on the subordination of one racial group by another' (1977: 35). Wellman's inflated definition refers therefore to beliefs or sentiments and practices which he considers to constitute racism, not on the basis of their content, but on the basis of their effects:

A position is racist when it defends, protects, or enhances social organisation based on racial disadvantage. Racism is determined by the consequences of a sentiment, not its surface qualities ... White racism is what white people do to protect the special benefits they gain by virtue of their skin colour. (Wellman 1977: 76)

What is common to the arguments of Blauner and Wellman is an inflation of the definition of the concept to include not only (or not so much) discourses (whether formal or disaggregated), but also (and more important) all actions and processes (whatever their origin or motivation) which result in one group being placed or retained in a subordinate position by another (cf. Williams 1985: 329-30). The concept of racism is used therefore to refer to a range of phenomena (beliefs as well as intended and unintended actions and processes) but with a specific emphasis upon their consequences for the domination of one group over another. These groups are defined, respectively, as 'black' and 'white', and consequently racism is conceived as something that 'white' people think about and do to 'black' people.

This inflation of the meaning of racism is accompanied by a complimentary narrowing which defines racism as an exclusively 'white' phenomenon. For Wellman, it is a matter of definition that only 'white' people express sentiments and act in ways which are defined as racism. This argument has been endorsed and developed by Katz, who argues not only that 'racism is a White problem in that its development and perpetuation rest with White people' (1978: 10) but that racism is a psychological disorder which is 'deeply embedded in White people from a very early age on both a conscious and an unconscious level' and which has 'deluded Whites into a false state of superiority that has left them in a pathological and schizophrenic state' (1978: 14-15). Thus the concept of racism refers not only to all actions or inactions, all sentiments and silences, which sustain 'black' subordination, but also to a form of schizophrenia, which all 'white' people 'have' in the sense that it structures the totality of their experience and being in the world. In sum, all 'white' people are universally and inevitably sick with racism.

These American theories have been as influential as they are controversial. The concept of institutional racism was noted by a number of British analysts in the late 1960s and early 1970s (Leech 1986: 85) and, since then, it has been used to analyse the British situation (for example, Allen 1973; Dummett 1973, Sivanandan 1982, Miles and Phizacklea 1984). Again, the use of the concept is explained in part by the historical context. Although explicit expression of theories of biological inferiority in the formal arena of politics was rare by the 1960s, descendants of those people who had been colonised and the subject of nineteeth century theories of 'race' had migrated from the colonial context to the 'mother country'. There they were concentrated in some of the worst housing and employed in largely manual jobs, despite the fact that certain forms of racial discrimination had also been declared illegal during the 1960s. Accordingly, attention began to turn away from explicit expressions of racism (*qua* ideology) and from intentional and individual discriminatory actions. As in the United States, the problem was identified as determining the cause of ongoing 'black disadvantage' and the meaning of racism was inflated to effect this task.

But the concept of institutional racism was introduced and used with little analytical rigour (Mason 1982, Williams 1985, Phillips 1987). For example, the term now occupies a central position in Sivanandan's writing (for example, 1982: 61, 84, 109, 113, 138) and yet he offers no formal definition. Although his analysis suggests that he draws a distinction between racism, institutional racism and racialism, these concepts are not defined and defended systematically. In an early paper, Sivanandan distinguishes between racism and racialism, using the former to refer to 'an explicit and systematic ideology of racial superiority' and the latter to refer to the unequal treatment of different 'races' (1973: 383). In a later set of essays, he defines racialism as simply attitudes and behaviour, and racism as the systematisation of these attitudes and behaviour into 'an explicit ideology of racial superiority and their institutionalisation in the state apparatus' (1982: 170n). Subsequently, he uses racialism to refer to racial prejudice and racial discrimination (1983: 2). More recently, racialism is defined as individual prejudiced attitudes, and racism as 'structures and institutions with power to discriminate' (1985: 27).

Within Sivanandan's analysis, the meanings of these different terms shift without explanation: at one point, racialism is used to refer to discriminatory treatment and at another to individual prejudice, while racism first refers to a particular and explicit ideology and later to those institutions with the power to discriminate. In this latter example, racism seems to have been equated with institutional racism and to refer to any institution with the power to discriminate rather than to a systematic ideology of 'race'. Viewed collectively, these writings demonstrate a transition to a conception (which is not always explicitly defined) of racism which uses the term to refer primarily, although not always exclusively, to institutional discriminatory practices. The concept of racism therefore focuses upon practices to the exclusion of ideology: 'It is the acting out of racial prejudice and not racial prejudice itself that matters ... Racism is about power not about prejudice' (Sivanandan, 1983: 3).

These arguments offer a very different concept of racism from that used by the writers considered in the previous section who defined it exclusively and specifically as an ideology. First, the concept has a generalised rather than a specific referent: it identifies as racism all those beliefs, actions and processes which lead to, or sustain, discrimination against and the subordination of 'black' people. Second, it denies that intentionality or motivation are measures of the presence or absence of racism. While an explicit motive or intention to subordinate may be evident, it is not considered to be a necessary condition for the identification of racism. Third, by definition, racism is a prerogative of 'white' people. Fourth, although there are important exceptions (such as Sivanandan 1983, 1985), it asserts or assumes a theory of stratification in which the terms 'white' and 'black' have analytical status. The social formation under analysis is identified as constituted by the presence of two (homogeneous) groups, 'whites' and 'blacks', which have a hierarchical relationship with each other. In that hierarchy, 'blacks' are a subordinated totality and totally subordinated while 'whites' are a dominant totality and totally dominant. By implication, the struggle between these two groups constitutes the primary, if not the sole, dynamic within the social formation. Thus racism is identified as the determinant of the continued and continuous domination of 'blacks' by 'whites'.

Elsewhere, I have evaluated critically this inflated concept of racism (Miles 1982: 72-9) and I elaborate on that critique here. First, the concept is inseparable from a theory of stratification that is simplistic and erroneous because it states or assumes that the sole or primary division within a society is between 'white' people and 'black' people. From the perspective of both

Marxist and Weberian theory, this suppresses or denies the existence of class divisions and conflict, and the distribution of 'white' and 'black' people to different class positions. Consequently, the simplistic definition of ('white') racism as 'prejudice + power' (such as in Katz 1978: 10) ignores the class divisions within the 'white' population, and hence the differential access to power amongst that population. Evidence of the extent of racist beliefs and sympathy for Fascist politics amongst sections of the 'white' unskilled working class in Britain (for example, Phizacklea and Miles 1980: 175) is therefore more accurately understood as a response to *inter alia* powerlessness rather than the possession of power.

The analytical problem is therefore more complex because racism is expressed within a structure of class differentiation and exploitation. Within European and North American capitalist societies, it is within the interstices of the conflicting interests of, and struggles between, the bourgeoisie, *petite bourgoisie* and working class (and their various fractions) that the effectivity of racism must be located. For this reason, I can agree with the spirit, although not the specific theoretical formulation, of Sivanandan's assertion that 'power is not something white people are born into, but that which they derive from their position in a complex race/sex/class hierarchy' (1985: 27).

Moreover, there is considerable evidence to demonstrate that 'black' people in the United States (for example, Wilson 1978: 19-22, 59-60, 152-4; but see Pinkney 1984, Omi and Winant 1986) and Britain (for example, Miles 1982: 176-84, 1987b) do not collectively constitute a homogeneous population, occupying a common economic position which is subordinate to that of all 'white' people. If racism is defined as the prerogative of 'white' people and as the consequence of any action which sustains the subordination of 'black' people, it is not clear how one can conceptualise and explain, for example, the continued situation of economic disadvantage of sections of the 'black' population in American cities where 'black' people occupy positions of power in the political administration (cf. Gurnah 1984: 12). Similarly, it is not clear how one can conceptualise the continued situation of economic disadvantage of (often female) 'black' employees of the small, but growing, 'black' bourgeoisie and *petite bourgeoisie* in Britain (see, for example, Hoel 1982, Anthias 1983, Mitter 1986). It could be claimed that, because those in positions of power are 'black', it follows by definition that their (conscious or unconscious) actions cannot be racist, but this contradicts the conceptualisation of racism as all those *acts* which have as their consequence the creation or maintenance of disadvantage. The reality of this problem is evident in, for example, Sivanandan's use of quotation marks when referring to the 'black' *petite bourgeoisie* (1985: 14), suggesting that when 'black' people occupy positions of political and administrative power within the state they become less 'black'.

Second, this concept of racism is ultimately teleological. If, as Katz argues, racism is a disease that all 'white' people 'have', and if racism is 'perpetuated by Whites through their conscious and/or unconscious support of a culture and institutions that are founded on racist policies and practices' (1978: 10), then all 'white' actions (and inactions) are racist. The definition is all-inclusive, with the result that, for example, if a 'white' person suggests that some particular act is not racist, this is interpreted as evidence of a 'delusion' because, by definition, all 'whites' and all acts which sustain the status quo are racist and all 'whites' are sick. In other words, the concept has no discriminatory power whereas the analytical objective of identifying a phenomenon as racism is to distinguish it by reference to specified criteria from others which do not exhibit those qualities and which therefore have the quality of 'not racism'. But in an inherently and holistically racist society, there can be no actions, other perhaps than the act of revolution (as long as the act is not carried cut by 'whites') which have this quality. The concept therefore assumes what should be demonstrated in every particular instance.

By this 'logic', this inflated concept of racism conflates explanation: the complexity of contradictory and interlocking, of structural and conjunctural processes are reduced to a single determinant, that is, all that 'white' people do to maintain their domination (cf. Williams 1985). For example, let us consider the well-documented fact that people of Caribbean and Asian origin in Britain are more likely to be unemployed than people of indigenous origin when the economy is in crisis and there is a shortage of jobs (for example, Smith 1977: 67-72, 1981: 2-6, Newnham 1986). There is firm evidence to demonstrate that this is, in part, the consequence of exclusionary practices based on negative stereotypes and an endorsement of a refusal of workers of indigenous origin to work with people of Caribbean and Asian origin (see Smith 1977: 170-81). However, in the 1980s, it has also been determined partly by the fact that workers of Asian and Caribbean origin are more likely to have been employed in the textile and clothing industries which are more vulnerable to restructuring and therefore abolition than others, as a result of which they have been overrepresented amongst those made redundant (Smith 1981: 34-5, Brown 1984: 154-5).

Moreover, it is necessary to explain why, despite a similar level of discriminatory treatment (Smith 1977: 111), certain sections of the Asian population have very low levels of unemployment (lower than for the population of indigenous origin) and certain sections of the Caribbean population have very high levels of unemployment (Barber 1985: 473-5, Anon. 1987: 27-8). In the British context, the category 'black' refers to what is in other respects (i.e. other than their collective experience of being identified as 'black') a heterogeneous population, a population composed of men and women, young and old, originating from different historical, colonial, and cultural contexts, with the result that different traditions and resources are available to these different groups, influencing (although not necessarily determining) their position and strategy within (and outside) the labour market. If racism is what 'white' people do, it tells us nothing about what different groups of 'black' people do in and outside the labour market, how they avoid, accommodate to, and resist the various structural and conjunctural determinants of unemployment and therefore influence whether or not they are unemployed. Formally, these must be considered as potential determinants of labour market position, with their effects being assessed comparatively with the effects of racism conceived as an ideology which structures exclusionary practices (Miles 1987b).

Finally, what is a collective disadvantage is not necessarily an individual disadvantage and, similarly, the determinant of the collective disadvantage is not necessarily the determinant of the individual disadvantage. Not all people of Asian and Caribbean origin in Britain are unemployed (indeed it is minority condition and experience: see, for example, Anon. 1987), and an explanation for their unemployment must be consistent with this fact. And although the evidence does demonstrate that active and intentional discrimination is a major determinant of Asian and Caribbean unemployment, considered individually, some instances will be explained by other factors such as, for example, physical disability and industrial injury.

It is, therefore, simplistic and misleading to argue that this specific disadvantage faced by people of Asian and Caribbean origin is a consequence of what 'white' people do. There is no single explanation for comparatively higher rates of unemployment amongst people of Asian and Caribbean origin, despite the impression so created by attributing the origin of the fact to racism. Additionally, it is simplistic and misleading because in a capitalist economy undergoing rationalisation and reorganisation, 'inefficient' sectors, factories and offices are likely to be closed down irrespective of who has the power to make the decisions and of who is employed within them. In this sense, defining the employers as 'white' might be true in the sense that they have a particular skin colour, but it could be irrelevant to the determination of the actual outcome. Redundancy and unemployment presume a combination of the operation of the criterion of profitability and the commodification of labour power, and these are therefore integral determinants of Asian and Caribbean unemployment, as they are of the unemployment of any other group of workers. Explanations which refer solely to racism ignore or deny this structural precondition and determinant of unemployment. My argument is therefore not one which seeks to minimise but one which seeks to *contextualise* the impact of racism.

Third, that racism is defined as a structural domination of 'black' by 'white' limits the scope of the analysis to certain historical instances and excludes a number of conjunctures in which, by another definition, a racist ideology has been expressed, the object of which were not 'black' people, in order to legitimate exclusionary practices. Thus, the history of European representations of the European Other is excluded from consideration. For example, in the nineteenth century, the Irish in Britain were widely defined as a distinct 'race', and although the stereotype of the Irish was not a consistently negative one, it was nevertheless a stereotype which attributed specific characteristics to the Irish 'race' in a deterministic manner (Curtis 1968, 1971, Walvin 1986: 93). As recently as the 1920s, an official report to the General Assembly of the Church of Scotland identified the Irish 'race' as a threat to the very existence of the Scottish 'race' and its positive cultural attributes, stereotyped the Irish as criminals, claimed that they were intending political domination, and called for controls over Irish immigration to Scotland (see Miles and Muirhead 1986). Historically, the idea of the Irish as an inferior 'race' was accompanied in Scotland by widespread violence against them as well as by active trade union opposition to the employment of the Irish and by discrimination against the Irish by employers (Miles 1982: 135-45). In turn, this has had significant effects upon the expression of racism in post-1945 Scotland (Miles and Dunlop 1986, 1987).

In the United States in the early twentieth century, a campaign for controls on the entry of certain European populations was organised on the basis of the attribution of an inferiority of 'race'. It was argued, citing evidence supplied by psychologists, that the population of Europe was made up of a number of different 'races', each of which had a different native or inborn intelligence, and that an increasing proportion of immigrants to the United States originated from southern and eastern Europe and were of inferior 'race'. In comparison with people of British, German and Scandinavian 'stock', Italian, Polish, Russian and Jewish immigrants were said to have a naturally inferior intelligence and their increasing presence in the United States was considered to lower the average level of intelligence. Dire consequences were predicted, and the Johnson-Lodge Immigration Act of 1924 was passed with the intention of preventing 'race deterioration' (Kamin 1977: 30-51, Gould 1984: 224-32).

Finally, there is the example of the use of the idea of 'race' to identify and exclude Jews. Throughout Europe in the nineteenth century, much older representations of the Jews as ritual murderers, as wanderers, and as conspirators with the objective of world domination were revitalised and given new force through the idea of 'race':

> The mystery of race transformed the Jew into an evil principle. This
> was nothing new for the Jew ... But in the last decades of the
> nineteenth century and the first half of the twentieth, the traditional

legends which had swirled about the Jews in the past were revived
as foils for racial mysticism and as instruments of political
mobilisation. (Mosse, 1978)

This mystical idea of 'race' was paralleled by, and sometimes integrated with
(as in the case of the writing of Houston Stewart Chamberlain), the science of
'race', both sustaining the idea of the distinctiveness of, and conflict between,
Aryan and Jewish 'races'. This representation was influenced by and found a
location in all the central ideological traditions of European thought, and
played a central role in the expression of different European nationalisms
(Mosse 1978, Biddiss 1975: 11, 1979a: 508-9).

But it was in Nazi Germany, in a wider context of economic and political
crisis, that the idea of the Jews as a degenerate, unproductive and criminal
'race', as simultaneously a 'race' of exploiters and revolutionaries (Mosse
1978: 178, 219), was a key factor in the evolution of a state policy of genocide.
For Hitler, 'race' determined culture and historical development, and he
identified the Aryan 'race' as chosen to rule the world, as the guarantor of
civilisation (Dawidowicz 1977: 44-8). The idea that the Aryan 'race' was
engaged in a struggle for survival with the Jewish 'race' was embodied in the
Nuremberg Laws of 1935. They were intended to maintain the purity of
German 'blood' in order to ensure the continued existence of the German
people, and made marriage and extramarital relations between Jews and
Germans illegal (Dawidowicz 1977: 98-101). Jews were declared in law to be
non-Germans:

> This legal definition, separating German Jews from Germans, laid
> the foundation for the liquidation of these 'parasites' who were
> poisoning the German blood and the German nation. Arguments
> invoking genocide were frequently phrased in terms of biological
> pollution and racial hygiene. (Seidel 1986: 21)

The significance of the science of 'race', supported by the Nazi state, was
evident in the continuation of anthropological measurements of Jews in the
concentration camps, alongside human vivisection, the subjects of which were
usually Jews (Biddiss 1975: 17, Mosse 1978: 227-8).

None of these three examples falls within the scope of a definition of
racism as all actions, intended or otherwise, by 'white' people which have the
consequence of sustaining their dominant position over 'black' people. Using
such a definition, they must be defined as instances of some other
phenomenon, despite the use of the nineteenth century, scientific idea of 'race'
and its legitimation of discrimination. By citing these examples, I am not
suggesting that they share precisely the same origins and causes with the

situation in the United States and Britain. Rather, my argument is that a concept of racism that is formulated by reference to a single historical example (the United States) and then uncritically applied to one other (Britain) has a degree of specificity that seriously limits its analytical scope.

The fourth problem with the inflated concept of racism is that, by defining racism as the consequence of what 'white' people do, the distinctions between belief and action, and between intentionality and unintentionality, are obscured. In the case of the concept of institutional racism, this is presented as a virtue insofar as it is argued that the intentionality or otherwise of actions is secondary to their consequences. The interrelations between belief and action, and between intended and unintended consequences are complex. Beliefs may not be accompanied by or give rise to logically appropriate actions, and actions may occur which are not consistent with beliefs. Actions can produce consequences which are consistent with motivations and intentions, but they often, if not usually, also have unanticipated outcomes. These 'inconsistencies' are present in all social life and give rise to major problems of methodology and for the determination of 'causality'. They are largely marginalised by the inflated concept of racism.

There are a number of reasons to object to this marginalisation. If disadvantage is the consequence of intentionality and of a belief in the existence and inferiority of certain 'races', rather being the unintentional outcome of decisions or taken-for-granted processes by people who do not hold such beliefs, distinct interventionist strategies will need to be employed in each case. In other words, if the determinants are different, so should be the responses intended to prevent them from occurring in the future. Moreover, where there is no consistent or logical connection between ideas and actions, an analysis of the prevalence of racist beliefs may prove to be a very unreliable guide to the extent of discriminatory behaviour, and vice versa. By defining racism broadly by reference to consequences, use of this inflated concept absolves the analyst (and political activist) from the often difficult task of identifying the particularities of the processes that create and reproduce disadvantage. The simple distinction between, for example, overt and covert racism does not by itself resolve this problem: to designate racism as covert does not by itself reveal the complex, contradictory interplay of the determinants of disadvantage and exclusion.

There are many forms and determinants of disadvantage. The claim that the concept 'racism' identifies all those actions that have 'black' disadvantage as their consequence includes a very large number of actions and processes. Moreover it assumes that these actions are in some way exclusive in that they occur only where 'black' people are present and therefore because of the meaning attached to their 'blackness'. The advocates of this argument explicitly assert the exclusive nature of racism when they argue that it refers to what 'white' people do to 'black' people. Where the concept of racism is used to identify certain negative beliefs about people defined as black and/or actions which intentionally exclude, there is a clear measure of the exclusivity of disadvantage.

But if the presence of certain beliefs and of intentionality are defined as irrelevant to the identification of racism, the problem of exclusivity is correspondingly intensified. For example, it is often argued that 'word of mouth' recruitment to jobs is an instance of institutional racism because, in a workplace where no 'black' people are employed, such a process will therefore exclude them, irrespective of the intention and beliefs of the employer. But such a procedure excludes individuals from any group which is not represented in the place of work. Thus, if women, Irish, or Jewish people are not present, then they too are excluded by this method of recruitment, and hence the practice of 'word of mouth' recruitment is not exclusive in its exclusion of 'black people'. There are analytical implications. Is therefore the exclusion of women, Jews, and Irish to be defined as institutional racism? If not, how are these instances to be conceptually differentiated? And if they are, by what logic does one identify institutional racism as a specific phenomenon when other people are also excluded by the identical practice?

In order to identify racism as an exclusive phenomenon, affecting only certain groups of people, it is essential to be able to demonstrate that the consequences are exclusive or cannot be explained by reference to some other characteristic of 'black' people which is shared with some other group or groups. In other words, if the presence of specific beliefs and of intentionality are not necessary criteria by which to identify racism, the dangers of making a spurious correlation are considerably increased. Hence, systematic comparative analysis is essential: it is necessary not only to demonstrate that 'black' people collectively are treated in a certain manner or experience a particular disadvantage, but also that that treatment and disadvantage are not experienced by any other group. Demonstrating that something does not happen to some other group is, methodologically, much more difficult than demonstrating that something does happen to one particular group, with the result that assertions that particular practices constitute an instance of institutional racism are often difficult to substantiate.

For these four reasons, the inflation (and conflation) of the scope of the concept of racism so that it refers to all beliefs and actions of 'white' people which ensure their domination over 'black' people is of limited analytical value. The broad and imprecise scope of the concept needs to be deflated in order to sharpen its analytical power and, as I shall subsequently argue, in so doing one can also retain the concept of institutional racism, but with a narrower and more precise meaning.

THE NEW RACISM

These difficult problems are largely avoided by a more recent conceptualisation of racism within the British literature which uses it to refer to a particular form of ideology. This definition returns to the problem of identifying the criteria by which one classifies whether or not a particular discourse warrants description as racism. In common with the previous two conceptions of racism discussed above, it too has a specific historical origin, this time in Britain, although there is an echo of certain arguments advanced by Frantz Fanon three decades earlier.

One of Fanon's central concerns was to demonstrate the effects of colonialism upon the colonised, partly in order to understand the implications for national development after successful anti-colonial struggle. In the course of so doing, he made a number of comments about the nature of racism and, in a paper written in 1956, he made three observations that have been more widely articulated in the recent past. First, he argued that racism is not a static phenomenon, but is constantly renewed and transformed, and second, that the primitive racism grounded in biological claims corresponded to a past phase of colonialism (partly because these arguments had been discredited by the consequences of Fascism in Germany). Third, he claimed that racism was a central aspect of colonial domination which, along with other mechanisms, was intended to transform colonised populations into the objects to be used for the purpose of the coloniser (Fanon 1970: 41-54).

What is less clear is Fanon's own definition of racism. The closest he comes to offering one is in the context of his suggestion that primitive racism has been replaced by cultural racism which has as its object not individual human beings but 'a certain form of existing' (1970: 42) and that racism 'is only one element of a vaster whole: that of the systematised oppression of a people' (1970: 43). It is therefore integral to colonialism which Fanon referred to as 'the conquest of a national territory and the oppression of a people' (1970: 91), although in his later text, *The Wretched of the Earth*, Fanon noted that racism was one of the 'pitfalls of national consciousness' in decolonised African nation states (1967: 125-31). We see here, therefore, another instance of conceptual inflation, as a consequence of which the concept of racism is expanded to refer broadly to a process of oppression (and therefore presumably to both ideology and practice), although how it is to be distinguished from other forms of oppression is never clarified.

In Britain, by the mid-1970s, the population of Caribbean and Asian origin originating largely from post-1945 migration had been resident for more than two decades and its numerical increase was due more to natural reproduction than to immigration. There emerged during this decade a 'new' political discourse within the British state which asserted that, as we have seen in the

Introduction, it is natural for people to prefer to live amongst 'their own kind' and therefore natural for people to discriminate against those not considered to be part of that common community. Such arguments either made no mention of, or in some cases specifically rejected, the idea of a hierarchy of 'races', thereby disengaging (at least explicitly) with that particular discourse of the Other which, as we saw in chapter 1, has a history which extends back to the late eighteenth century. This discourse was labelled by Barker as the 'new racism' (1981).

Barker argued that the new racism emerged in Britain as part of a broader revision of Conservative Party ideology in the wake of the defeat of the Conservative government of 1970-4. One dimension of this revision focused on immigration, which was regarded as having brought to Britain a population which destroyed the cultural homogeneity of the British nation and which, as it grew in size, was identified as threatening to 'swamp' the culture of 'our own people'. Thus, Barker identified the 'core of the new racism' as:

> a theory of human nature. Human nature is such that it is natural to form a bounded community, a nation, aware of its differences from other nations. They are not better or worse. But feelings of antagonism will be aroused if outsiders are admitted ... Each community is a common expression of human nature; all of us form exclusive communities on the basis of shared sentiments, shutting out outsiders. (Barker 1981: 21-2)

Identifying this theory of human nature as a form of racism, Barker recognised that it is necessary to define the general category of racism. In doing so, he claimed that

> the prevalence of a definition of racism in terms of superiority/ inferiority has helped conceal how common is a form of racism that does not need to make such assertions - indeed, can make a positive virtue out of not making them. It is indeed a myth about the past that racism has generally been of the superiority/inferiority kind. (Barker 1981: 4)

Theories and arguments are identified as racism if they see 'as biological, or pseudo-biological, groupings which are the result of social and historical process' (1981: 4).

The idea was taken up by a number of other writers working within the Marxist tradition, most notably by a group who wrote *The Empire Strikes Back* in the name of the Centre for Contemporary Cultural Studies (CCCS 1982: 27, 29, 48, see also Gilroy 1987). As with Barker, their focus is upon a particular emergent ideology within the Conservative Party, an ideology which is seen to be an integral part of a wider ideological realignment within the Party in the context of the development of an organic crisis of British capitalism. This ideology is seen largely, although not exclusively, to dispense with a notion of biological superiority/inferiority, and to formulate a notion of the Other as being naturally different in cultural terms and to have a natural 'home' outside Britain. There is much that is similar here with Barker's analysis. What is less clear than in Barker's analysis is their definition of the concept of racism.

The CCCS text offers a description of the nature of racism but does not identify any criteria by which racism can be distinguished from any other ideology. It is argued that it is not a fixed, static ideology but is contradictory and constantly undergoing transformation (1982: 9-11). It is said to have deep historical roots, so that ideas and arguments derived from an imperialist history are continually being reworked and given new meanings as a result of contemporary endogenous political-economic forces, and combined with new ideas and images (1982: 11-12, 48, 66, 68, 70, 74). But no attempt is made to identify the characteristics that would permit it to be identified as racism: many, if not all, ideologies are flexible and fluid and many, if not all, have a historical chronology, and so these criteria do not permit us to identify what is distinctive about *racism* as an ideology.

Indeed, if, as the text argues, racism is always in a process of transformation, it is particularly important to identify the criteria by which this ever-changing ideology can be identified. Presumably there must be some transhistorical features which identify the different racisms as instances of a specific form of ideology, distinct from other ideologies such as nationalism and sexism, for example, but we are never advised what they might be. Additionally, the CCCS text assumes, but fails to demonstrate, that the arguments of a small number of individuals in the Conservative Party are hegemonic, reduces the parameters of contemporary British racism to the arguments of this small group and, most importantly of all, operates with an (undefined) conception of the new racism which is derived from a single empirical instance.

The work of this CCCS collective is influenced by the work of its previous Director, Stuart Hall (1978, 1980). For example, the former's claims, that contemporary British racism has been shaped by endogenous forces and that there is no single, static phenomenon of racism (1982: 9-12), are repetitions of assertions made previously by Hall (1978: 24, 26, 1980: 337). In turn, Hall echoes arguments expressed much earlier by Fanon. And the reluctance of the CCCS collective to specify the analytical content of the concept of racism is also shared with Hall (and with Fanon). Thus, Hall recognises that racism is a concept (a 'rational abstraction') that identifies a particular phenomenon but warns against 'extrapolating a common and universal structure to racism, which remains essentially the same, outside of its specific historical location' (1980: 337). However, if there are 'historically-specific racisms' (1980: 336), they must also have certain common attributes which identify them as different forms of racism. For example, capitalist social formations are similarly historically-specific, but they also share certain common attributes, and hence the 'rational abstraction', capitalism, which refers to those social formations characterised by *inter alia* generalised commodity production and the commodification of labour power. Hall does not specify what the many different racisms have in common *qua* racism.

Nevertheless, implicit in his argument is a use of racism which refers to ideology. He identifies racism as 'one of the dominant means of ideological representation through which the white fractions of the class come to "live" their relations to other fractions, and through them to capital itself' (Hall 1980: 341). He recommends an investigation of the 'different ways in which racist ideologies have been constructed and made operative under different historical conditions ... In each case, in specific social formations, racism as an ideological configuration has been reconstituted by the dominant class relations, and thoroughly reworked' (1980: 341-2). In his analysis of British indigenous racism, Hall examines the way in which the 'black' presence is identified as 'the enemy within', as the signifier of the crisis of British society. He explains: 'This ideology, which is formed in response to a crisis, must of course, to become a real and historical political force, connect with the lived experiences of the "silent majorities" ' (1978: 30). Hall therefore uses the concept of racism in a narrower sense than that employed in the analytical tradition founded in events in the United States in the 1960s. Moreover, his suggestion that the analytical task is to identify the historically-specific racisms (and their real material conditions of existence) constituted the theoretical groundwork for the specification of the 'new racism' by Barker and its use by the CCCS collective.

In comparison, Barker's analysis has the virtue of explicitly defining racism, although it is a problematic definition (Miles 1987c). In order to define the arguments of a particular faction within the Conservative Party as an instance of racism, Barker inflates the definition so as to refer to all arguments which mistakenly identify a group as being a biological or pseudo-biological entity when it has been constituted socially. Thus, nineteenth and twentieth century arguments which assert that, for example, the French people have a natural set of common characteristics which justify their constituting a nation state is an instance of racism. And so is the claim that women are the weaker sex. In other words, Barker's definition of racism eliminates the distinction between racism and, respectively, nationalism and sexism.

He is also mistaken in his claim that racist ideologies have not generally asserted a hierarchy of superiority and inferiority. The historical material in chapter 1 demonstrates clearly that a large proportion of European and North American representations of the Other have asserted a hierarchy of superiority/inferiority, certainly since the sixteenth century and probably earlier, although these have not always been expressed in terms of inherent biological differentiation. Nevertheless, identification with the Christian religion was a crucial component of the establishment of a hierarchy of the saved and the damned within Europe, as well as a legitimation of a war with the Islamic world. And, significantly, Barker cites no examples to sustain his case. For these, and other reasons (see Miles 1987c), the concept of the new racism is problematic because the definition of racism is problematic.

CONCLUSION

Considered historically, the concept of racism has had a relatively short career during which its analytical definition has been expanded in two directions. On the one hand, a number of writers have continued to confine the use of the term to refer to specific discourses, but have inflated its meaning to include ideas and arguments which would not be included by those who initially formulated and used it. Thus, there is a logical connection between the British debate about the definition of racism in the late 1960s and the debate about the new racism in the 1980s. Both debates reflect the fact that, at least within the formal political domain, claims about the existence of biologically inferior and superior 'races' have largely disappeared, but a discourse of the Other continues with a new ideological content. On the other hand, other writers have inflated the analytical meaning of the concept so as to refer largely to individual and institutionalised practices which have as their outcome the determination and/or reproduction of 'black' disadvantage, regardless of intention and legitimating ideology. Hence, discourses of the Other are either largely irrelevant or secondary to this analytical position.

Why has this analytical inflation occurred? Or, to put it another way, why have so many writers resisted Banton's rejection of the concept on the grounds that the ideology that the concept originally referred to is 'dead'? There are two (interrelated) reasons, one analytical and one political. The first is that, seen from a particular theoretical perspective, the long history of the interdependence of capitalist development and 'black' subordination began a new chapter with the migration of 'black' people from the peripheries of capitalism (whether they be overseas colonies, as in the case of Britain and other European nation states, or the southern agricultural plantations in the case of the United States) to the metropolitan centres. Within the peripheries of capitalism in the eighteenth and nineteenth centuries, the exploitation of 'black' labour power in unfree relations of production placed 'black' people in a subordinate position to the emergent proletariat at the centre and was legitimated by representations of the Other which identified those so exploited as belonging to biologically inferior 'races'.

Consequently, an analytical interdependence of capitalism and racism was established. Hence, following migration, when it became apparent that the commodification of 'black' labour power was accompanied by subordination 'below' the position occupied by the majority of 'white' labour power (evident in the concentration of 'black' wage labourers in the poorest quality housing and in semi- and unskilled manual labour, for example), it was concluded that the essential structure of 'black' subordination had not changed, even if the ideological justification had. The point of emphasis became the continuity of 'black' structural subordination rather than ideological transformation, and consequently the meaning of the concept of racism was inflated in order to take account of this.

And this brings us to the second factor, for the decision to inflate the definition of racism must have an explanation. From a radical, and certainly from a Marxist, point of view this transformation sustained the argument that linked racism and capitalism in some sort of causal dependency. Thus, the political critique of capitalism could be broadened and capitalism could be damned for yet another reason. Morally, this critique was sustained by the horror and outrage concerning the holocaust, which ensured that the word racism took on a new sense of disapproval after 1945. There were therefore good political and moral reasons to continue to employ the concept because it carried with it a strong negative evaluation. To label someone or something as an instance of racism was to place the person or event outside the boundaries of civilisation.

However, this theoretical and political perspective is not sacrosanct. Indeed, it is problematic for two reasons. First, the essential continuity perceived is open to question. The migration from periphery to centre was not only a spatial migration but also often a movement from one (non-capitalist) mode of production to another (capitalist) mode of production and hence from one set of class relations to another. And, within the capitalist mode of production, the complex interdependence of capital accumulation, bourgeois individualism, commodification, and relative freedom from relations of personal dependence (the equation between female gender and domestic labour is a central exception) creates opportunities for at least some of those people previously directly subordinated by colonisation and unfree relations of production to move into a number of different class locations.

Second, much of the British and North American theorising about capitalism and racism since the 1960s, while drawing upon the immoral status of racism which derives to a significant degree from the final solution, utilises a colonial model which has little scope to explain much of the European racism of the nineteenth and twentieth centuries, and certainly not that form of racism which others label anti-semitism (for example, Cox 1970: 393-4); it does, however, have a relevance to the controversial debate about whether or not Zionism can be defined as an instance of racism (see Kayyali 1979). Consequently, we are offered definitions and theories of racism which are so specific to the history of overseas colonisation (that is, specific to the domination of 'white' over 'black' as so many writers express it) that they are of little value in explaining any other (non-colonial) context.

3

On signification

INTRODUCTION

In the light of the problems identified in the previous chapter, it is necessary to reconsider the definition of the concept of racism. This will involve a clarification of the relationship between the concept of racism and a number of related concepts. These are the central objectives of this chapter. They will be realised by reflecting theoretically on the nature of the social process by which meanings are attributed to real or imagined human biological characteristics. Thus, a concept of racism will be derived analytically rather than inductively from consideration of a single empirical instance (such as Nazi ideology and practice, or British colonialism). But this theoretical work will produce no more than a *concept* of racism. It will therefore identify what many different instances of racism have in common *qua* racism, but it will tell us nothing about the specificity of each instance. That is, it will not identify the variety of representational content or the circumstances that structure the determination of that content and its expression. These are matters for historically specific analysis, examples of which will be discussed in chapter 4.

'RACE'

The theoretical work begins with the idea of 'race', from which the concept of racism was initially derived. We have seen that racism was first used to identify the Nazi theory of 'Aryan' superiority and Jewish inferiority which was derived in part from nineteenth century scientific theories of 'race'. Consequently, the concept of racism has been assumed to refer exclusively to theories of 'race'. That is to say, the presence of the discourse of 'race' is a precondition for the identification of racism. The first objective of this chapter is to break this conceptual link between racism and the discourse of 'race' in order to substantiate an analytical use of the concept of racism.

The word 'race' continues to be used in at least three different discourses in the English speaking world. Within the world of science, it appears in the discourse of the biological sciences, specifically genetics, and of the social sciences. Additionally, it is widely used in everyday (including political) discourse, and constitutes a key element of common sense (the accumulated, taken-for-granted, and often contradictory set of assumptions and beliefs that are employed by people to impose an ideological structure upon the social world, within which they can then act). These uses are differentiated, yet interrelated.

Within genetics, debate continues about the validity of using an 'old' concept to refer to a 'new' phenomenon, that is to the patterns of genetic variation which are not observable to the eye and do not correlate with evident phenotypical variation. Although it is certain that the scientifically legitimate object of analysis has changed from phenotypical difference to genetic variation, there is no unanimous view that this transition should be reflected in a change in scientific terminology so that the term 'race' is no longer used to refer to populations differentiated by average frequencies of specific polymorphic genes (Miles 1982: 18-19, also Montagu 1964: 23, Jones 1981). Certainly, there is no scientific justification for using the term to refer to a discrete hierarchy of 'races' as distinguished by phenotypical features such as skin colour. In the latter sense, as far as the biological and genetic sciences are concerned, 'races' do not exist (see Montagu 1972; Rose *et al*. 1984: 119-27).

However, in the everyday world, the facts of biological differentiation are secondary to the meanings that are attributed to them and, indeed, to imagined biological differentiation. In order to understand the significance of this, it is necessary to explore briefly the meaning of the concept of signification. I use the concept to identify the representational process by which meanings are attributed to particular objects, features and processes, in such a way that the latter are given special significance, and carry or are embodied with a set of additional, second-order features (cf. Potter and Wetherall 1987: 24-8). Signification therefore involves selection: from an available range of objects, features and processes, only certain ones are chosen to convey additional meanings. The object, feature, or process treated in this way thereby becomes a sign of the existence of some other hypothesised or real phenomenon. Signification is therefore a central moment in the process of representation, that is, the process of depicting the social world and social processes, of creating a sense of how things 'really are'.

Where the discourse of 'race' is employed, there are two levels of selection involved in the process of signification. The first is the selection of biological or somatic characteristics in general as a means of classification and categorisation. The second is a selection from the available range of somatic characteristics those which are designated as signifying a supposed difference between human beings. Human beings actually differ from each other phenotypically on a wide range of characteristics, including for example height, weight, length of arms and legs, ear shape, width of feet, breadth of palm, hair colour, extent of body hair, and so on. Thus, when the idea of 'race' is employed, it is the result of a process of signification whereby certain somatic characteristics are attributed with meaning and are used to organise populations into groups which are defined as 'races'. People differentiated on the basis of the signification of phenotypical features are usually also represented as possessing certain cultural characteristics, with the result that the population is represented as exhibiting a specific profile of biological and cultural attributes. The deterministic manner of this representation means that all those who possess the signified phenotypical characteristics are assumed to possess the additional cultural characteristics. Further, it follows that the human species is conceived as consisting of a number of distinct collectivities, and each single individual is attributed with membership of one of those collectivities.

In Europe, North America, and Australasia, the idea of 'race' is now usually (although not exclusively) employed to differentiate collectivities distinguished by skin colour, so that 'races' are either 'black' or 'white' but never 'big-eared' and 'small-eared'. The fact that only certain physical characteristics are signified to define 'races' in specific circumstances indicates that we are investigating not a given, natural division of the world's population, but the application of historically and culturally specific meanings to the totality of human physiological variation. This is made equally evident when we consider the historical record which demonstrates that populations now defined as 'white' have in the past been defined as distinct 'races'. Thus, the use of the word 'race' to label the groups so distinguished by such features is an aspect of the social construction of reality: 'races' are socially imagined rather than biological realities.

These processes of signification and representation have a history. Chapter 1 demonstrates that, within Europe, somatic characteristics have been signified for several centuries as a means of representation of human beings, and that skin colour has been commonly selected from the range of somatic features as the primary sign by which the Other can be created. The use of the discourse of 'race' to refer to the populations differentiated by somatic characteristics is, however, more recent. While this form of representation has been discredited scientifically, the fact that the idea of 'race' continues to be employed in common sense testifies to its continuing practical rather than scientific utility. Husbands has commented: '"Race" as a means of categorising people theorises the "social facts" of colour difference in a rigid and absolute way which carries all the implicit naturalness and authority of "race"-thinking' (1982: 16). The signification of phenotypical features is therefore not an end in itself but is effected for particular purposes. Hence, as I shall argue shortly, its practical utility is not simply representational but is also a means to effect exclusionary practices, with the result that patterns and structures of material inequality between populations so differentiated are created in the context of class differentiation.

Since the early part of this century, a 'school' of North American and European social scientists has defined the study of this and consequent processes as the scientific study of relations between 'races' or 'race relations' (for example, Banton 1977: 101-11, 1987: 86-93, Rex 1970, 1986, George 1984). Since the early 1970s, the definition of this field of study has been broadened to include 'ethnic' as well as 'race relations'. As I have argued elsewhere (Miles 1982: 22-43, 1984a, 1988a), these writers have employed uncritically the common-sense notion of 'race', reified it and then attributed it with the status of a scientific concept. Similarly, Guillaumin has argued:

> Whatever the theoretical foundations underlying the various interpretations of 'racial' relations, the very use of such a distinction tends to imply the acceptance of some essential difference between types of social relation, some, somewhere, being specifically racial. Merely to adopt the expression implies the belief that races are 'real' or correctly apprehensible, or at the best that the idea of race is uncritically accepted; moreover it implies that races play a role in the social process not merely as an ideological form, but as an immediate factor acting as both determining cause and concrete means. (1980: 39, see also Lecourt 1980: 282-3)

Thus, social scientists (including many who define themselves as Marxists: see Miles 1988b) have, perversely, prolonged the life of an idea that should be explicitly and consistently confined to the dustbin of analytically useless terms.

But if 'race' was a European discourse projected onto various Others, it has not remained a discourse of subordination. During the twentieth century, those who have been its object have often accepted their designation as a biologically distinct and discrete population, as a 'race', but have inverted the negative evaluation of their character and capacities. Consequently, the discourse of 'race' has been transformed into a discourse of resistance. Certain somatic characteristics (usually skin colour) have been signified as the foundation for a common experience and fate as an excluded population, irrespective of class position and cultural origin, as a result of which a political appeal to 'race' (commonly in the form of an appeal to 'blackness') is made in order to effect a political mobilisation intended to reverse material and political disadvantage as well as colonial rule. One of the most well-known instances is the rise of the Black Power movement in the United States in the 1960s (see Seale 1970). The political content, objective and strategy of such mobilisations vary considerably, but they all have in common at least an implicit acceptance of the legitimacy and accuracy of the European discourse by means of which they have been constituted as an Other. Indeed, the inversion of the negative evaluation serves to reinforce at a deeper level the process of signification by which the Other was originally constituted (cf. Fanon 1967: 188-9, Chachage 1988) and therefore, in the course of resistance, the discourse of 'race' is further legitimated.

Clarity of meaning is vital here. It is not denied that there are somatic and genetic differences between human beings. Neither is it denied that phenotypical (and sometimes genetic) characteristics are signified in the 'real world' as indicative of meaningful differences between human beings, and that at a certain historical period the idea of 'race' was employed to name the collectivities so distinguished. What is at issue is the scientificity of the terms that are used to analyse this representational process, this historical construction and reproduction of common sense in the European world, and its economic and political consequences. If 'races' are not naturally occurring populations, the reasons and conditions for the social process whereby the discourse of 'race' is employed in an attempt to label, constitute and exclude social collectivities should be the focus of attention rather than be assumed to be a natural and universal process. Hence, the construction and reproduction of the idea of 'race', is something that requires explanation. This task is circumvented by transforming the idea itself into an analytical concept. Thereby, what needs to be explained and represented as a social process is reconstructed as a social fact which is presented as explaining other social facts.

On the matter of my critique of 'race relations' sociology (Miles 1982, 1984a, 1988a), I have nothing further to add here. I now regard the generation of the concepts with which one can grasp and portray in a consistent manner the historicity of this process as a more important analytical task. In particular, because 'race' and 'race relations' are ideological notions which are used to both construct and negotiate social relations (and hence their use in quotation marks throughout this text), the concepts that are employed to analyse that social process should reflect that fact consistently. Only then will we have a scientific language that allows the deconstruction of the idea of 'race' rather than a language which reifies, and thereby legitimates, it.

RACIALISATION

The first key concept is 'racialisation'. Again, brief consideration of the origin of the concept is relevant to the specification of its meaning. It was first used by Fanon in a discussion of the difficulties facing decolonised intellectuals in Africa when constructing a cultural future (1967: 170-1). Banton (1977: 18) utilised the concept more formally to refer to the use of the idea of 'race' to structure people's perceptions of the world's population. His usage was limited, and by implication, its scope was confined to referring to the way in which scientific theories of racial typology were used to categorise populations. More recently, Reeves has distinguished between 'practical' and 'ideological' racialisation, using the former to refer to the formation of 'racial groups' and the latter to refer to the use of the idea of 'race' in discourse (1983: 173-6, see also Troyna and Williams 1985). This is an extension of Banton's use of the concept, not only by virtue of drawing this distinction but also because his concept of ideological racialisation refers to any circumstance where the idea of 'race' is employed in discourse. Hence, Reeves analyses the way in which the discourse of 'race' has entered British political discourse and, in turn, has been reified in legislation since 1945. Omi and Winant use the concept to 'signify the extension of racial meaning to a previously racially unclassified relationship, social practice or group. Racialisation is an ideo- logical process, an historically specific one' (1986: 64). This definition corresponds closely to Reeves' concept of practical racialisation.

In these various usages, there is minimal agreement that the concept be used to refer to a representational process whereby social significance is attached to certain biological (usually phenotypical) human features, on the basis of which those people possessing those characteristics are designated as a distinct collectivity. Banton and Reeves both specify that such a process only occurs where the collectivity is explicitly defined as a 'race'. Thus, for these two writers, the process of racialisation begins with the emergence of the idea of 'race', and continues for the duration of the employment of the idea of 'race' to categorise the world's population (cf. Guillaumin 1980: 49).

Elsewhere, I have used the concept of racialisation as a synonym (1982: 120, 150) for the concept of 'racial categorisation' which I have defined as 'a process of delineation of group boundaries and of allocation of persons within those boundaries by primary reference to (supposedly) inherent and/or biological (usually phenotypical) characteristics. It is therefore an ideological process' (Miles 1982: 157). For reasons of analytical clarity, I prefer now to use only the concept of racialisation, but defined as above in order not to limit its application to historical contexts where the idea of 'race' is present. Hence, we again confront the problem that was discussed when considering the parameters of the concept of racism in chapter 2, namely whether or not to limit the use of the concept to a discourse in which the idea of a hierarchy of 'races' is present.

I do not impose such a restriction. This is because, as I have shown in chapter 1, phenotypical characteristics such as skin colour have been signified within European social formations to constitute in thought discrete collectivities prior to the introduction of the idea of 'race'. For example, within the Greco-Roman world, the African's skin colour was signified as a means of collective representation, and a similar process occurred during the period of European exploration from the fifteenth century. In other words, the idea of 'race' has a pre-history, during which time the representation of the Other was effected through the signification of certain physical features which were subsequently identified as the criteria by which a person's 'race' was supposedly determined. Similarly, in much contemporary discourse in Europe and North America, categories such as 'white' and 'black' are used to label individuals, and hence to constitute groups, but often in the formal absence of the discourse of 'race'.

I therefore employ the concept of racialisation to refer to those instances where social relations between people have been structured by the signification of human biological characteristics in such a way as to define and construct differentiated social collectivities. The characteristics signified vary historically and, although they have usually been visible somatic features, other non-visible (alleged and real) biological features have also been signified. The concept therefore refers to a process of categorisation, a representational process of defining an Other (usually, but not exclusively) somatically. The defined collectivity is considered (implicitly if not explicitly) to constitute a naturally occurring, discrete breeding population and therefore subsumes a pattern of gender differentiation. The concept of racialisation, by highlighting the process of categorisation as one of attributing meaning to somatic characteristics, presumes a social psychological theory which explains the nature and dynamics of the process (for example, Billig 1976: 322-69).

Racialisation is a dialectical process of signification. Ascribing a real or alleged biological characteristic with meaning to define the Other necessarily entails defining Self by the same criterion. When the Greco-Romans and later the northern European explorers and merchants defined Africans as 'black', they were implicitly defining themselves as being at the opposite end of a common dichotomy or continuum, that of skin colour. The African's 'blackness' therefore reflected the European's 'whiteness': these opposites were therefore bound together, each giving meaning to the other in a totality of signification. Similarly, when Africans were later identified as constituting an inferior 'race' by Europeans, Europeans were simultaneously, if only implicitly, defining themselves by reference to the discourse of 'race', albeit with a different evaluative connotation. Thus, Self and Other were similarly encapsulated in a common world of (European) meanings. By virtue of sharing in that common world of meaning, the Other may adopt the content of the racialised discourse to identify itself as Self. Thus, the European discourse of 'race' has become accepted by those populations whom it was used to exteriorise and exclude as a legitimate discourse by which to identify both Self and Other. In so doing, the evaluative content has often been changed from a negative to a positive value.

A periodisation of the process of racialisation would identify the emergence and utilisation of the idea of 'race' as the central (but not the sole) phase in its history. Since the eighteenth century, as we saw in chapter 1, the world's population has been sorted in European thought into 'races', and relations between 'races' were thought to be shaped, if not determined, by their supposedly inherent characteristics. Moreover, even if the idea of a hierarchy of 'races' is no longer articulated in the formal political arena, it is still widely assumed that 'races' exist as distinct, biologically defined, collectivities. Thus, the idea of 'race' continues to be widely employed as a universal descriptive category in order to designate collectivities to which both Self and Other belong. The concept of racialisation therefore refers to the historical emergence of the idea of 'race' and to its subsequent reproduction and application.

Furthermore, the racialisation of human beings entails the racialisation of the processes in which they participate and the structures and institutions that result. Thus, where human beings are identified as collectivities by reference to physical features, the interrelations between those collectivities will be effected in part by means of, for example, extant political institutions and processes. This is dramatically evident where 'races' are defined in law as discrete collectivities and where the law actively structures the relations between those collectivities (as in South Africa) but it also occurs where somatic signification is effected and negotiated through less formal mechanisms. Consequently, issues such as who occupies positions of leadership and the topics that are placed on the political agenda may come to be shaped by the meanings attributed to phenotypical variation: thus, demands may be made that 'black' people be represented within decision-making structures or that 'white kith-and-kin' should be given a privileged status in immigration law. In such circumstances, the political process is racialised in the sense that it takes on a particular representational content by representing 'race' as the determinant and object of political relations.

In sum, I use the concept of racialisation to refer to a dialectical process by which meaning is attributed to particular biological features of human beings, as a result of which individuals may be assigned to a general category of persons which reproduces itself biologically. This is a process which has a long history, and has occurred in precapitalist and capitalist societies. The particular content of the process of racialisation, and its consequences (including its articulation with political and economic relations), cannot be determined abstractly or derived formally from the primary features of the mode of production but are matters for historical investigation, as we shall see below and in chapter 4.

RACISM

The second key concept is racism. Its short history leaves us with a complexity of meaning and usage which requires clarification. I offer a clarification in two main stages. First, I argue that the concept should be used to refer exclusively to an ideological phenomenon. Then, and second, I identify the specific representational characteristics that must exist to warrant description as racism.

The case for limiting the use of the concept to refer exclusively to ideology is based on the assumption that the analytical value of a concept is determined by its utility in describing and explaining societal processes. The inflation of the meaning of the concept has resulted in it being used to refer to not only ideologies but also to a very wide range of practices and processes. As I have argued in the previous chapter, not only does such a concept have very little discriminatory power, but it also makes the identification of determinacy difficult. Moreover, there is no necessary logical correlation between cognition and action. The conceptual ability to make these distinctions is necessary not only in the interests of analytical accuracy but also, and therefore, in the interests of formulating potentially successful interventionist strategies intended to negate both racist ideologies and the disadvantage that accrues from exclusion.

Before elaborating on this complex duality between cognition and practice, it is necessary to clarify the concept of 'exclusionary practice' which I use to analyse all instances where a specified group is shown to be in unequal receipt of resources and services, or to be unequally represented in the hierarchy of class relations. For example, in the instance of contemporary Britain, it refers to the statistical fact that children of manual workers are underrepresented amongst university students (Halsey *et al.* 1980: 176-94), to the fact that male youths of West Indian origin are overrepresented amongst the unemployed (Newnham 1986: 17-20) and to the underrepresentation of women in management positions (Oakley 1981: 150-62). The fact of unequal representation or receipt of rewards and services presumes the existence of decisions and processes which discriminate between people but also the existence of scarcity: acts of discrimination and exclusion are premised on the need to allocate scarce resources and services and therefore involve decisions of worth or eligibility.

Hence, and first, the concept of exclusionary practice refers only to a concrete act or process and does not presuppose the nature of the determination, the specification of which requires independent investigation. It does not presuppose, for example, that the exclusionary practices which determine the experience and position of people of African origin in the United States or of Caribbean and Asian origin in Britain result, either partially or exclusively, from the signification of, and attribution of negative meanings to, their skin colour. This requires demonstration by means of comparative analysis. For example, as I have already shown, high rates of unemployment amongst Afro-Americans in the United States or people of Caribbean and Asian origin in Britain, for example, may be at least partially due to their overrepresentation in sectors of employment which are especially vulnerable to 'rationalisation' rather than to intentional exclusion based on the signification of somatic features. In order to avoid the interrelated dangers of supposing that the explanation for disadvantage is mono-causal and that the disadvantaged position of 'black' people is necessarily consequent upon racialisation, it should be assumed that exclusionary practices have a number of determinants.

Second, the concept of exclusionary practice refers to both intentional actions and unintended consequences which create patterns of inequality. Both the actions and the consequences must prevent individuals from gaining access to some service or position, or lead to their overrepresentation in some negatively evaluated category (such as being stopped and searched by the police). It therefore includes both calculated attempts to achieve inequality as well as a complex of decisions and actions which unknowingly result in inequality (although where the latter is shown to occur, a subsequent decision not to revise the practices and procedures constitutes an intentional action). For the purpose of analytical clarity, as well as to determine strategies of intervention, it is important to ascertain whether exclusionary practices result from either intentional or unintentional actions.

Third, there is a dialectical relationship between exclusion and inclusion, and in two senses. Acts or processes of exclusion which, for example, prevent people of Caribbean and Asian origin from gaining paid employment in Britain serve to define, implicitly if not explicitly, the criterion by which others are included, that is, the characteristics of those who do gain access to jobs. Moreover, acts or processes of inclusion which, for example, led to an over representation of children of West Indian parents in 'special schools' for the educationally subnormal in Britain (Coard 1971) were simultaneously acts and processes of exclusion of such children from 'normal schools'. In both senses, inclusion and exclusion refer to different moments in a single act or process: to include is simultaneously to exclude and vice versa.

But if the concept of racism is more narrowly defined as a representational phenomenon, distinguished from that of exclusionary practice, what are its primary defining characteristics? In chapter 2, I argued that it should be identified by its ideological content rather than by its function. The distinguishing content of racism as an ideology is, first, its signification of some biological characteristic(s) as the criterion by which a collectivity may be identified. In this way, the collectivity is represented as having a natural, unchanging origin and status, and therefore as being inherently different. In other words, a process of racialisation must be occurring. Second, the group so identified must be attributed with additional, negatively evaluated characteristics and/or must be represented as inducing negative consequences for any other. Those characteristics may be either biological or cultural. Thus, all the people considered to make up a natural, biological collectivity are represented as possessing a range of (negatively evaluated) biological and/or cultural characteristics. It follows that such a naturally defined collectivity constitutes a problematic presence: it is represented ideologically as a threat (cf. Miles 1982: 78-9).

The ideology of racism has a number of additional characteristics. First, because it presumes a process of racialisation, it has a dialectical character in so far as the representation of the Other serves simultaneously to refract a representation of Self. If the Other is a naturally constituted collectivity, then so must Self be. Racism is therefore a representational form which, by designating discrete human collectivities, necessarily functions as an ideology of inclusion and exclusion: for example, the signification of skin colour both includes and excludes in the process of sorting people into the resulting categories. However, unlike the process of racialisation, the negative characteristics of the Other mirror the positive characteristics of Self. Racism therefore presupposes a process of racialisation but is differentiated from that process by its explicitly negative evaluative component.

Second, racism may take the form of a relatively coherent theory, exhibiting a logical structure and adducing evidence in its support, but it also appears in the form of a less coherent assembly of stereotypes, images, attributions, and explanations which are constructed and employed to negotiate everyday life. Too many of the contributions to the debate about the nature of racism as an ideology have an intense fascination with the writing of fellow intellectual practitioners but an almost complete ignorance of the way in which representations of the Other have been created and reproduced in the daily life of the working class. Racist assertions can be coined as easily in the factory or office as in a university library. One of the major limitations of the original concept of racism was therefore that its object was largely textual, and this was reflected in the definition of racism as a doctrine. Historically, when compared with the massive stock of racist literature produced by journalists, missionaries, retired army officers, 'amateur' scientists and university professors (for example, Biddiss 1979b; Gregory 1925), we have only limited evidence of the nature and extent of racist ideologies amongst the working class.

Hence, and third, racism is practically adequate (for discussion of this concept, see Sayer 1979: 3-11) in the sense that it refracts in thought certain observed regularities, and constructs a causal interpretation which can be presented as consistent with those regularities and which serves as a solution to perceived problems. An emphasis upon racism solely as a 'false doctrine' fails to appreciate that one of the conditions of existence of ideologies (which by definition constitute in their totality a false explanation, but which may nevertheless also incorporate elements of truth) is that they can successfully 'make sense' of the world, at least for those who articulate and use them. Put another way, the ideology of racism can constitute for some sections of a population a description of and explanation for the way in which the world is experienced to work. And because racism is practically adequate, at least part of its content will vary with the class position of its exponents because the world as it is experienced and the problems that are created vary with class position.

This can be demonstrated with two examples. During the nineteenth century, the competitive preeminence of British capital ensured that the British bourgeois and merchant capitalist classes occupied a position of unrivalled economic and political domination within the capitalist world economy. The productive and technological superiority of British capitalism, especially when supported by an equally superior military machine, was especially evident when its representatives and advocates were engaged in a further expansion of the British Empire in Africa and India in the nineteenth century. There was, in other words, a real material difference between the conditions of the British bourgeoisie and merchant capitalists and the populations of Africa and India where petty commodity production was either hardly evident or had been partially, if not wholly, destroyed by the combined activities of the former classes and the system of production that sustained them.

That difference, which was experienced as real, required explanation. An argument that the British bourgoisie was part of (if not the preeminent members of) an inherently superior 'white race', with a biological capacity for invention, democracy and the spread of 'civilisation' to those less fortunately endowed by nature (and God), not only justified colonial strategies (Thornton 1965) but, perhaps more importantly, actually made sense of the world as it was experienced, even if it was non-sense. The falsity of the ideology was in inverse proportion to its effectivity for sections of the British ruling class as an explanation for a real material difference between populations and classes living within a single world economic system dominated by the capitalist mode of production. Moreover, it was an account of the world which additionally recognised and offered an explanation for the (long-established) signification of certain real physical differences between coloniser and colonised. Indeed, the idea of 'race' served to link the observed, real material differences and signified phenotypical differences in a total, causal explanation (Miles 1982: 113-19, cf. Curtin 1965: 293-4, Cairns 1965: 147-8). This ideology was reproduced throughout Britain by a wide variety of cultural forms, including the theatre, school text books, comics, films, novels and advertising (see Street 1975, MacKenzie 1984).

A second example is found in the few British studies of the way in which racism refracts the experience of the world, and therefore the contradictory consequences of capitalist development, by sections of the working class (Phizacklea and Miles 1979, 1980: 173-5, Miles and Phizacklea 1981; for a similar argument, see Cashmore 1986). These studies demonstrate that racism helps to make sense of the economic and social changes accompanying industrial and urban decline as they are experienced by sections of the working class. In many areas of working-class residence in Britain, the decline of capitalist production and the decay of the urban infrastructure (both inevitable features of the uneven development of capitalism) coincided temporally with the arrival and settlement of migrants from the Caribbean and the Indian subcontinent. While the determinants (rather than the consequences) of the changing composition and mobility of capital and the long-term failure of capitalism to provide sufficient, adequate housing for the working class were not immediately, visibly evident, the presence of populations signified historically as inferior 'races' was, and remains so.

The consequence has been that the facts of economic decline and migrant settlement have been experienced as causally related by sections of the indigenous working class. Thus, a real problem of exclusion from access to material resources and services, and the search and struggle for a resolution of that problem has been racialised. The idea of 'race' is used to define the Caribbean and/or Asian migrants as an illegitimate, competing Other whose presence has either caused or intensified the struggle for housing, social services, and employment, from which it is concluded, apparently logically, that the problems could be resolved by excluding the Other. For this reason, working-class racism does not have to be explained by proposing a capitalist conspiracy or by identifying small groups of people who gather to celebrate Hitler's birthday and who can only see Jews and 'black' people as biologically degenerate. Rather, it seeks a significant part of the explanation in the active attempt to interpret and explain the world as experienced by sections of the working class.

This evidence gives empirical substance to Hall's theoretically derived assertion that the expression of racism within the working class is a form of representation by which sections of the working class live out their experience of the capitalist mode of production (1980: 341). It confirms more generally that racism

> is not a set of mistaken perceptions ... [It arises] because of the concrete problems of different classes and groups in the society. Racism represents the attempt ideologically to construct those conditions, contradictions and problems in such a way that they can be dealt with and deflected at the same moment. (Hall, 1978: 35)

In other words, racism can successfully (although mistakenly) make sense of the world and thereby provide a strategy for political action for sections of different classes. It follows that to the extent that racism is an attempt to understand a specific combination of economic and political relations, and is therefore grounded in those relations, strategies for eliminating racism should concentrate less on trying exclusively to persuade those who articulate racism that they are 'wrong' and more on changing those particular economic and political relations.

Fourth, as defined above, the concept of racism does not identify a specific historical content. Rather, it identifies the general characteristics that a discourse must possess to qualify as an instance of racism. In other words, racism is not a single, static ideology, one that is identified by the persistence of a specific set of assertions, images, and stereotypes. Empirically, there 'have been many significantly different racisms - each historically specific and articulated in a different way with the societies in which they appear' (Hall 1978: 26, also 1980: 342). Again, the importance of this can be illustrated by recent as well as historical research.

Returning to the limited body of research on the nature of working class racism, Annie Phizacklea and I have emphasised the specificity of the racism that we identified amongst some of the working class in London in the 1970s when we noted the relative insignificance of stereotypes derived from Britain's history as a colonial power (Phizacklea and Miles 1979: 97-8, 119-20, 1980: 173-4, also Thurlow, 1980). It was not that the imagery of, for example, 'black savagery' was absent. It was sometimes articulated as contextualisation, but it was of little value in explaining the economic and political realities of a shortage of housing and a variety of social facilities and services in London in the 1970s (although it may have a greater utility in explaining the representation of West Indian male youth as especially prone to criminal assault). The specific racism that we identified in that context was one in which skin colour served to identify the Other, and the Other was considered to have a privileged and illegitimate access to resources (for example, Phizacklea and Miles 1979: 111).

The fluidity of racism can also be demonstrated historically. Jordan's (1968) immensely detailed account of the changes as well as the continuities in American representations of the African illustrates this in a masterly fashion. Drawing on this and other work, I have shown in chapter 1 that most European and North American representations of Africans in the eighteenth century considered them, like Europeans, to be human beings but nevertheless a distinct human being, distinguished by skin colour but also *inter alia* by a potent sexuality, bestiality, and laziness, all of which were negatively evaluated. Consequently, the African was ranked below the European on a hierarchy of acceptability. During the nineteenth century, the idea of 'race' assumed increasing prominence, and accordingly there was an important change in the representation of the African as Other. Many of the negatively evaluated characteristics continued to be attributed to the African but the over-all nature of the African when compared with the European was re-evaluated.

Thus, skin colour, potent sexuality, and bestiality, etc. were no longer thought to be either environmentally determined or evidence of degeneration but were considered to be amongst the inherent characteristics of the African 'race'. This was a racism which represented the African as essentially different from the European and therefore confined the African as Other to inferiority in perpetuity, unlike that of the eighteenth century which presented the African as a form of deviation from a (European) norm and which assumed that the attributed inferiority was a temporal condition.

In response to specific events during the nineteenth century, there were significant shifts in the content of British representations of the colonised Other. The Indian Mutiny of 1857 had a profound impact upon British conceptions in both India and Britain. The predominant representation of the population of India had been that of a docile, industrious Hindu, but in the immediate aftermath of the mutiny the Indian was represented increasingly as deceptive, fanatical, and cruel. The image of the scheming, blood-thirsty Oriental was not new (it has a long history as we have seen in chapter 1) but was more widely articulated (and elaborated by the addition of the image of the Indian as 'nigger') in an attempt to comprehend the events of 1857 and to justify the imposition of direct British rule over India. Although in the longer term, the (contradictory) myth of the effete Hindu persisted, the ideological reaction to the events of the mid-nineteenth century in India demonstrated the fluidity of racism, the responsiveness of its articulators to real events and the ability creatively to reshape the ideology.

Similarly, events in the Caribbean in the mid-nineteenth century provided an occasion for a change in British representations of the African, although this took the form of a simple reinforcement of existing representations. The Jamaican revolt of 1865 was widely interpreted as evidence of the innate savagery and inferiority of the African 'race' and for the need for strong government in order to prevent a retreat into barbarism: the association of the African with savagery and barbarism in the European mind also has a long history, as we have seen, but the events of 1865 strengthened the view in the British public mind that these were biologically determined characteristics (Bolt 1971: 102-8, 178-205, 209-10).

Thus, racisms differ on a number of dimensions. The group that is identified as its object, the natural features signified, the characteristics attributed to the group and negatively evaluated – all of these aspects of racism are historically variable. But they are not historically random. While it is important to identify and explain the dynamic content of racism, its fluidity, there are also certain historical continuites. Again, as I have shown in chapter 1, certain European representations of the African have remained prominent for long periods of time. Different racisms are therefore not necessarily independent of each other, are not continually created anew in any absolute sense. Rather, any one instance of racism will be the product of both a reworking of at least some of the substance of earlier instances, and a creation of novel elements.

In sum, I use the concept of racism to refer to a particular form of (evaluative) representation which is a specific instance of a wider (descriptive) process of racialisation. As a representational phenomenon, it is analytically distinguishable from exclusionary practices. Such a distinction is essential to the task of explanation because it does not foreclose the identification of the reasons why racialised populations occupy disadvantaged positions in contemporary or past social formations. Having demonstrated that a racialised population has been intentionally or unintentionally excluded from, for example, the labour market, it does not follow that this is the consequence, wholly or in part, of racism. Exclusionary practices may be partially or wholly motivated by or expressive of racism, but this must always be demonstrated rather than assumed to be the case.

INSTITUTIONAL RACISM

A third key concept is 'institutional racism'. For the reasons stated in the previous chapter, I find the original, broad definition of this concept to be of limited utility. However, I believe that a case can be made for the retention of the concept with a more precise definition so that it refers to two sets of circumstances. First, there are circumstances where exclusionary practices arise from, and therefore embody, a racist discourse but which may no longer be explicitly justified by such a discourse. Seccnd, there are circumstances where an explicitly racist discourse is modified in such a way that the explicitly racist content is eliminated, but other words carry the original meaning.

What both circumstances have in common is that the racist discourse becomes silent, but is nevertheless embodied (or institutionalised) in the continuation of exclusionary practices or in the use of the new discourse. The continuing practice or the new discourse is expressive of an earlier, racist discourse. Hence, the concept of institutional racism does not refer to exclusionary practices *per se* but to the fact that a once present discourse is now absent and that it justified or set in motion exclusionary practices which therefore institutionalise that discourse. An ideology of racism is thereby embodied in a set of practices, but this warrants classification as institutional racism only where the process of determinacy can be identified. Thus, in order to determine the presence or otherwise of institutional racism, one assesses not the consequences of actions but the history of discourse in order to demonstrate that prior to the silence (or to the transformation), a racist discourse was present.

Both of these forms of institutional racism can be illustrated by a British example, the first by reference to immigration law (for example, Macdonald 1983). None of the post-1945 British Immigration Acts employs an explicitly racist discourse: they do not make explicit reference to 'black' people and they contain no statement of intent to exclude people defined as a distinct 'race' (unlike, for example, the Special Restriction (Coloured Alien Seamen) Order of 1925: see Rich 1986: 122-30, Gordon and Reilly 1986). Nevertheless, when the political context in which the legislation was passed is examined, we find that a racist ideology was present and that the legislation was introduced in order to realise racist objectives.

During the late 1940s and early 1950s, the British government used various administrative devices to restrict the entry of 'coloured' Commonwealth citizens, and even secretly considered introducing legislation to prevent their entering and settling in Britain, which was then their right. During the late 1950s, and especially after the attacks on people of Caribbean origin in 1958, there were increasing demands from politicians to restrict the rights of entry of these Commonwealth citizens because, it was alleged, they were more likely to engage in criminal acts and to be carrying contagious diseases. There was public pressure to restrict 'coloured' immigration from the electorate because it assumed dire consequences for housing and state benefits; increasingly supported by MPs, this was sufficient to allow the Conservative Government to legislate in 1962 in the way that had been desired a decade earlier (see, for example, Joshi and Carter 1984, Miles and Phizacklea 1984, Miles 1984b, Harris 1987, Carter, Harris and Joshi 1987).

All subsequent legislation has been intended to ensure that the objectives of the 1962 Act are more effectively achieved. Thus, the 1968 Commonwealth Immigrants Act by a clever legal device withdrew the right of 'coloured' UK passport holders to enter Britain, while the 1971 Immigration Act extended the right of entry and settlement to several million 'white' people. A key feature of the political context for this legislation of the late 1960s and early 1970s was the prominence of Enoch Powell MP, who, in a series of speeches, carefully racialised the people of Asian and Caribbean origin in Britain and alleged a range of negative consequences for 'our own people' arising from their presence in Britain (Smithies and Fiddick 1969, Schoen 1977, Miles 1988a). Additionally, the state's own legitimation of its legislation that came to predominate in the 1960s, but which was emergent in the late 1950s, is a prime instance of a racialised discourse that contributed to the institutionalisation of racism.

The legitimation claimed that 'strict immigration control was essential to ensure good race relations'. This maxim alleged that, as a result of immigration, a number of different 'races' were living in Britain and that in order to ensure that they could co-exist without conflict, the numerical presence of the 'races' that had recently entered Britain had to be limited. This was because, in the words of a Government White Paper *Immigration from the Commonwealth* published in 1965, 'the presence ... of nearly one million immigrants from the Commonwealth with different social and cultural backgrounds raises a number of problems and creates various social tensions in those areas where they have concentrated.' The immigrant presence was therefore the cause of problems which would have to be solved, 'if we are to avoid the evil of racial strife and if harmonious relations between the different races who now form our community are to develop'. Hence, the discourse which paralleled and legitimated immigration legislation was explicit in confirming the strategy of withdrawing from certain 'races' the right of entry to Britain because they created social problems.

This maxim illustrates the second instance of institutional racism, the racist discourse that is subsequently embodied in an apparently non-racist discourse. During the 1950s, those MPs agitating for immigration legislation were explicit in demanding that the legislation apply exclusively to 'coloured people'. In this respect, they were only demanding what we now know that the first two post-war governments were considering doing: the Cabinet papers are quite explicit on this point (Joshi and Carter 1984, Carter, Harris and Joshi 1987). However, in the light of the (accurate) accusation of racism, such explicit references became less common in the formal statements of politicians who increasingly referred only to the need for 'firm immigration control'. Given that the original agitation had explicitly identified 'coloured immigrants' as constituting a problematic presence and, given that immigration continued to be represented as creating a 'race relations' problem, the apparently more neutral language of 'immigration' and 'immigrant' therefore carried a set of implicit meanings or a subtext. As a result, they were understood to refer specifically to 'coloured' immigrants. One interesting instance of this coding is the way in which, during the late 1960s, opinion poll questions eliciting views on the 'repatriation' referred sometimes to 'immigrants' and sometimes to 'coloured immigrants' (Miles 1988a). This coding is also central to the discourse of the New Right, as I have demonstrated in the Introduction.

The concept of institutional racism therefore refers to circumstances where racism is embodied in exclusionary practices or in a formally non-racialised discourse. But, in both cases, it is necessary to demonstrate the determinate influence of racism. As I have already argued, exclusionary practices that result in disadvantage for racialised groups cannot be assumed to be determined wholly or in part by racism.

IDEOLOGICAL ARTICULATION

The final concept that I employ is that of 'ideological articulation'. By this I mean that ideologies may share a common content or generalised object which allows them to be joined together or interrelated, to be expressed in ways in which elements of one are incorporated in the other. It is a concept which highlights the overlapping, juxtaposition, and contiguity of ideologies.

As an ideology, racism shares certain characteristics with others which results in their articulation. The central shared characteristic is the mistaken postulation of natural divisions within the human species which are defined as inherent and universal. These divisions are therefore presented as inevitable determinants of social organisation. As a result, certain institutions and processes are presented as timeless, as unalterable, and those who advise to the contrary are seen to wish to reverse the irreversible. This is a secularised version of divine will: the idea of God is replaced by the idea of Nature (although in some versions of this argument, Nature is seen to be a production of divine will). In both cases, a power independent of human beings is represented as a determinant of social relations. Such a representation involves reification for the institutions, and processes created and reproduced by human beings are refracted in thought as 'real things' with power over them (Lukács 1971: 83-109, Marx 1972: 818-31).

The two most important ideologies with which racism articulates are sexism and nationalism. All depend on a process of signification and can be used to effect inclusionary and exclusionary processes. In the case of sexism, real biological, sexual characteristics are identified as absolute differences, and are associated in a deterministic manner with a number of additional (real and attributed) biological and cultural characteristics in order to identify two essentially different categories of human being, men and women. In other words, differences of sex serve as the foundation for the construction of gender. Femininity and masculinity are represented as a collection of essentially different qualities inherent in women and men, from which conclusions are then drawn about their respective, differential participation in economic and political relations. Gender is therefore a social construction (Barrett 1980: 84-113) by which men and women are represented as naturally different categories of person. Sexist arguments additionally claim that these supposed differences explain and justify the differential and inferior treatment of women. The articulation between sexism and racism, and its consequences for our understanding of class relations, has recently become a matter of discussion (for example, Davis 1982, Anthias and Yuval-Davies 1983) and has begun to be explored in the debate about the significance of racism within the feminist movement (for example, CCCS 1982: 212-75, Amos and Parmar 1984, Mama 1984, Barrett and McIntosh 1985, Bhavnani and Coulson 1986).

One basis for the articulation of racism and sexism is the biological capacity of women to bear children. The signification of this capacity, and the subsequent confinement of the task of child-rearing to women, has served to exclude women from a wide range of economic and political activities in a large number of historical contexts. One consequence of this exclusion has been to represent women as, and ensure that they function as, breeding machines, a representation and confinement that links in a most significant way with the process of racialisation, on the grounds that biological reproduction is central to the task of reproducing 'races'. Thus, in historical contexts where migration and populations of migrant origin have been racialised, considerable concern about the implications for women has been expressed by all classes in the interests of preventing what has been defined as 'racial degeneration'.

The practical consequences are various. Where migrants have been recruited to fill a temporary shortage of labour, single men have been recruited on a contract basis and women have been excluded absolutely in an attempt to prevent the settlement and reproduction of an 'inferior race'. In historical contexts where a colonising population has been anxious to constitute and reproduce itself as the dominant 'race' in the interests of 'civilisation', it has often encouraged the migration of women of the same 'race' in order to increase the size of the colonising population by means of an increased birthrate (see MacKenzie 1984: 160). Both of these instances of articulation between racism and sexism were evident in nineteenth century Australia (de Lepervanche 1987) where the impetus for colonisation was represented as a masculine project: 'Physically proficient men, white and preferably British, were regarded as the best colonisers whose forceful nature, competitiveness and even occasional resort to brutality against inferiors were regarded as virtues to be applauded' (Evans, 1975: 10).

Less attention has been given to the articulation between racism and nationalism, although there are recent signs of an increasing interest (for example, Nairn 1981, Anderson 1983, Wright 1985, Miles 1987d). The ideology of nationalism similarly asserts the existence of a natural division within the world's population, a division between collectivities each with a distinct cultural profile and therefore a distinct capacity for constituting a self-governing nation state within a given geographical space. This ideology was a creation of the late eighteenth century, and was closely related to the political resistance to monarchic and aristocratic government in Europe (Smith 1983: 23, Kedourie 1985: 9-19). It posits 'nations' as universal entities, each with its own character and destiny. And because each 'nation' is defined as a unit which is capable of reproducing itself over time, it presumes, but does not always specifically identify, a presence of women and men. Consequently, there is a basis for the articulation between nationalism and sexism.

Elsewhere, in order to demonstrate the close correspondence between nationalism and racism as formal, nineteenth century ideologies, I have applied Anderson's suggestion (1983: 15-16) that the 'nation' constitutes an imagined community

> Like 'nations', 'races' too are imagined, in the dual sense that they have no real biological foundation and that all those included by the signification can never know each other, and are imagined as communities in the sense of a common feeling of fellowship. Moreover, they are also imagined as limited in the sense that a boundary is perceived, beyond which lie other 'races'. (Miles 1987c: 26-7)

Consequently, 'nations', like 'races', are the product of human invention (Hobsbawm 1983: 13-14). In Anderson's terms, the central difference between nationalism and racism lies in the former's additional claim that the 'nation' can only express itself historically where it occupies exclusively a given territory wherein the 'people' can govern themselves. No similar political project is explicit in the ideology of racism.

The ideas of 'race' and 'nation' are therefore both supra-class and supra-gender forms of categorisation with considerable potential for articulation. That potential was reinforced by the development of scientific racism from the eighteenth century. In its most extreme form, it argued that 'race' determined both cultural capacity and historical development, and it therefore followed that each 'nation' was the expression of a particular biological capacity. This was an articulation in which 'race' was 'nation'. Such an articulation was clearly expressed in the writings of Gobineau (1970: 164) who was a key figure in the development of scientific racism in Europe. But it cannot be concluded from the argument that there is a close logical articulation between nationalism and racism that an articulation occurs in every historical instance.

These ideologies are not independent and autonomous forces but are generated and reproduced within a complex interplay of historically constituted economic and political relations. The articulation between nationalism and racism is therefore historically specific and contingent. Elsewhere (1987c: 32-40), in a somewhat schematic manner, I have demonstrated the articulation between racism and nationalism in the case of England where, by the early nineteenth century, an earlier myth of Anglo-Saxon origin had been subsumed in an idea of 'race'. Consequently, it was widely believed that the English were largely an Anglo-Saxon 'race' characterised by an inherent capacity for freedom and for an ability to create democratic institutions, capacities which they could express in many other parts of the world (Horsman 1976, 1981: 9-77, MacDougall 1982).

The concept of 'ideological articulation' serves to highlight the contiguity of the ideology of racism. This is of special significance in the context of the conceptual inflation undergone by the concept of racism. Whereas some writers have continually expanded the analytical scope of the concept so that it includes discourses of exclusion which have previously warranted categorisation as instances of nationalism or sexism, I am suggesting that more attention could be usefully devoted to analysing the manner in which the ideology of racism articulates with other ideologies. In the rest of this chapter, I consider at greater length one historical instance of this articulation, and in so doing, I also illustrate the significance of the other concepts introduced and defined in this chapter.

THE ARGUMENT ILLUSTRATED

There has been some recent interest in comparing the nature and expression of racism in Britain and Australia (for example, Graves 1986, Yuval-Davies 1986). While the stimulus to this has been recent events in Australia, there are good reasons to open up a historical perspective on this comparison. As we have already seen, during the 1960s and 1970s, the British government passed legislation which institutionalised racism in the practice of immigration control, and in so doing, it mirrored the policy and practice established in the late nineteenth and early twentieth centuries by governments of a number of other Commonwealth countries. In the British settler colonies of Australia, New Zealand, Canada and South Africa, a capitalist mode of production was introduced during the second half of the nineteenth century (Denoon 1983), a process that was accompanied by the emergence of a merchant and industrial bourgeoisie that sought political self-determination. To this end, an ideology of nationalism was articulated which partially transformed the myth of the biological superiority of the Anglo-Saxon 'race' in order to create a sense of imagined community that was spatially and culturally distinct from its parent.

In the case of Australia, the ideology of racism was central to the development of that specific instance of nationalism.

There was not, in other words, an opposition between nationalism and racism (Anderson 1983: 136), but rather an interdependence such that the parameters of each ideology overlapped to determine the criteria for membership of the emergent nation state. The criteria of signification included the white 'races' as acceptable members of the Australian 'nation' and simultaneously excluded people of Asian and Pacific origin, who were represented as 'coloured races'. *Inter alia*, it was argued that people of the Anglo-Saxon 'race' had a special capacity for self-government by constitutional means, from which it was concluded that those not so biologically endowed should be excluded. Thus, the idea of the Anglo-Saxon 'race' sustained a belief in a sense of superiority of both 'race' and 'nation' (Huttenback 1976: 15-17).

This articulation developed in the course of a transition from what was a convict settlement with few, if any, commercial interests to the formation of a number of distinct colonies, each dominated by merchant and commodity producing interests. The articulation was most pronounced in the political debate leading up to the formation of the Commonwealth of Australia in 1901, the outcome of which was an exclusionary practice that ensured that the imagined community of Australia would consist exclusively of members of the 'white races'. The 'White Australia' policy, formally established in 1901, was not the outcome of a particular set of representations, but derived from a complex economic and political struggle between different fractions of capital and labour over migration flows into the Australian colonies, flows that were intimately connected with various initiatives to sustain and increase the supply of labour power as commodity production increased after the 1830s (McQueen 1970: 43-7, de Lepervanche 1984: 54). The consequence was a racialisation of migration flows and of immigration policy.

The Australian continent was sparsely populated prior to European settlement and the Aboriginal population proved resistant to incorporation into the emergent capitalist relations of production, with the consequence that a continuing migration was necessary to sustain the formation of proletarian and *petit-bourgeois* classes. Migration flows from Europe did not consistently meet the demand, and those seeking labour were regularly involved in initiatives to recruit labour from elsewhere in the world, and often under relations of unfreedom, for example, indenture (see Miles 1987a). It is in the context of the struggle to create a labour force 'willing' to provide labour power that we can locate the articulation between nationalism and racism.

During the early period of European settlement, the local state and many settlers anticipated that the Aboriginal population would serve as manual labourers within the economic relations that they were establishing (Reynolds,

1972: 109). However, the nature of Aboriginal production and social relations militated against any simple form of incorporation and the eventual consequence was widespread conflict and, after the successful assertion of European military technology and sheer numbers, the extensive although not total disintegration of those economic and social relations (Rowley 1970). This process was readily comprehensible in terms of the Darwinian notion of the survival of the fittest, and the Aboriginal population became widely regarded amongst the European settlers as a 'doomed race' (Evans *et al.* 1975: 85-90).

This representation overlay an often more complex interrelation between the economic and social relations of European settlement and the Aboriginal population, evident in certain regions for certain periods in the incorporation of Aboriginal labour power in various forms of production (Evans *et al.* 1975: 112, Miles 1987a: 105-12). Nevertheless, the prevalent image of the Aborigine amongst the European population remained a racist one. A combination of marginalisation and extermination placed the vast bulk of the Aboriginal population both materially and conceptually at or beyond the fringe of the social relations accompanying the development of commodity production in the Australian colonies. Thus, the debate about the nature of the imagined community of Australia rarely considered the original inhabitants of the continent.

A different process operated with respect to the Asian populations and the Pacific islanders who entered the Australian colonies in the nineteenth century. The rise of pastoralism, initially in New South Wales, from the third decade of the nineteenth century was accompanied by a recurring shortage of labour as convict labour and free migration from Europe proved unable to meet demand, and various private initiatives were made to recruit labourers from India and China under indenture to serve as shepherds (Willard 1967, de Lepervanche 1984: 37-42). The discovery of gold led to a significant increase in the migration of male labourers from China to work in the goldfields in the 1850s and again in the 1870s, and this presence aroused considerable opposition, following which restrictive legislation relating to the entry of Chinese was passed (Crawford 1923: 56-75, Willard 1967: 21, 24, 32-3). Willard suggests an interdependence of the economic and the ideological in the following passage:

> The heterogeneous mass of humanity on the Australian goldfields had objected to the presence of an exclusive and, in their opinion, an inferior Asiatic race - especially an 'inferior' people that proved able to mine so successfully as the Chinese. (Willard 1967: 35)

With the development of cotton and sugar production in Queensland in the 1860s, there was another initiative to recruit labour under indenture from

India, but this source was by-passed when the landowners found they could indenture labour from the Pacific Islands. Consequently, Pacific islanders were the main source of manual labour for the Queensland sugar industry in the late nineteenth century (Saunders 1982). There was considerable hostility towards these indentured migrant labourers who, as with the Chinese, were regarded as an economic threat by other sections of the working class and were signified as an 'inferior race'. Additionally, the fact that they were recruited under terms of indenture (unfreedom) was seen as a threat to the development of bourgeois democratic processes. One consequence of the hostile agitation was legislation to confine Pacific islanders to employment in tropical agriculture (Evans *et al*. 1975: 178-80).

With various examples of exclusionary legislation operating in the separate colonies, there was growing political awareness of the need for an immigration policy (a euphemism for exclusionary practice) that would apply throughout the continent. The practical significance of such a measure was well understood in the light of the experience of Chinese migrants entering one colony from another overland after legislation had been passed to restrict entry through the ports. Political pressure for unified action intensified during the 1890s and by the middle of the decade the various colonial governments were agreed on the need for some general restriction on the entry of 'coloured races' into the colonies. An intercolonial conference meeting in 1896 resolved that such a policy be implemented and thereafter three colonial governments published 'Coloured Races Restriction and Regulation' Bills (Willard 1967: 108-10).

The underlying racist agitation which sustained, and was legitimated by, this move increased the pressure upon the political leadership of the separate colonies to move towards federation (Palfreeman 1972: 136). The Attorney-General of the first Federal Government later commented

> No motive power operated more universally on this Continent, or in the beautiful island of Tasmania, and certainly no motive power operated more powerfully in dissolving the technical and arbitrary divisions which previously separated us than the desire that we should be one people, and remain one people, without the admixture of other races. (cited in Willard 1967: 119)

The demand to keep out 'coloured inferior races' was dialectically linked with an emerging sense of an imagined community of Australians, a collectivity that signified 'whiteness' as a sign of superiority and of inclusion.

This move towards an explicit ban on the entry into Australia of 'all coloured races' was, as far as the London government was concerned, sympathetically received in private and, because it was formally committed to a liberal policy of equality of peoples, a source of embarrassment in public. A Colonial Office memorandum commenting on the Conference expressed sympathy with the desire of the Australian colonies to avoid the 'permanent presence of a considerable element of an inferior race' (cited in Yarwood 1962: 263). But in the interest of maintaining its public image, the British government disallowed the planned legislation. However, it helpfully offered an alternative mechanism of exclusion which had the same effect but was achieved by a less explicit means. The model was the measure introduced in Natal in 1897 when entry into the colony was made dependent upon a proven facility with the English language (Huttenback 1976: 139-41, Palfreeman 1972: 137). The so-called 'Natal formula' was formally adopted and implemented in Australia in the 1901 Immigration Restriction Act which institutionalised racism in Australian immigration law and established an exclusionary practice effected by the state.

While the fact of exclusion and the sequence of events may not be subject to dispute, the significance and explanation for the racialisation of the Chinese, Asian, and Pacific island migrants, and hence the characterisation of the nature of the 'White Australia' policy have been. Willard (whose book was first published in 1923) argued that 'the validity and the morality of Australia's policy seems to depend on the validity and the morality of the principle of nationalism' (1967: 206) and that the fundamental reason for the 'White Australia' policy was the 'preservation of British-Australian nationality' (1967: 189). The denial that racism was a fundamental motive behind the 'White Australia' policy was echoed by writers in the 1950s who argued that it resulted from either an accurate and justifiable resistance by the emergent working class to the use of cheap labour by employers (Dallas 1955: 52) or from the expression of patriotism (Nairn 1956: 18-19).

The central error in this debate has been the presentation of the issue in simplistic 'either/or' terms. Attempts to represent the process of determination as one in which either the economic or the ideological factor was the sole 'cause' are mistaken because they fail to appreciate the complex totality of economic, political and ideological relations which led to the 1901 Immigration Restriction Act. My interpretation is that the development of commodity production and the formation of a proletariat in the various Australian colonies sustained the articulation and reproduction of the ideology of racism; this had its own determinant effects in association with the ideology of nationalism in the subsequent political debates about the form that the Commonwealth of Australia should take.

The articulation of nationalism and racism is inadvertently demonstrated in Willard's defence of the 'White Australia' policy as an exclusive and legitimate expression of nationalism. Willard appeared to argue that equality of treatment and cultural homogeneity were essential to the successful formation of a democratic nation state and that this was guaranteed by the 'White Australia' policy. An appeal was thereby made to an ideology (of nationalism) that had positive connotations and that was widely expressed in Europe. Consequently, the issue was presented as a legitimate desire by an imagined (homogeneous) community to express its unique character in the formation of a democratic nation state in which every person was equal. But Willard's advocacy of this principle of nationalism simultaneously expressed a belief in the existence of different, discrete 'races', each with a distinct set of characteristics and capacity for incorporation into a democratic nation state.

The primary theme of the argument was that 'racial unity is essential to national unity' (1967: 189, 207), a claim that was premised on the belief that Asian and Pacific island migrants were different 'races'. Willard claimed that these migrants were 'unfitted to exercise political rights, and incompetent to fulfil political duties' (1967: 193), and, specifically, that Asians had abilities which made them 'dangerous competitors' (1967: 197-8). Moreover, compared with the European 'race', these 'races' were not only different but also inferior. For example, she argued that the continued use of Pacific islanders as a source of labour under relations of indenture 'could be nothing else but the deliberate commercial exploitation of an inferior by a superior race' (1967: 197).

Moreover, Willard hypothesised that the permanent residence of such 'races' or 'alien people' in Australia 'would have a bad social effect on the community' (1967: 9). She argued, referring to Australians, 'The well-marked social and political evil inevitably connected with the co-existence of distinct races in one country, constantly recurred to their minds, and influenced them to take the first steps in the development of the policy' (1967: 192). The main example cited by Willard was that these 'alien peoples' were a source of cheap labour which caused competition, and this in turn

> would be a sure cause for racial strife, for it would arouse a primary instinct to fight for the right to existence such as Australians conceived it. It would acutely sharpen and intensify the political and social differences resulting from racial division. (1967: 200)

Indeed, for Willard, 'instinct' was the ultimate defence of the 'White Australia' policy

> In view of the feeling existing in Australia - the instinctive shrinking from racial admixture with peoples of strongly marked divergent ideals and physical characteristics - national unity would at present be an impossibility if non-Europeans were freely admitted. (1967: 207)

And, in order to sustain the claim that this was a universal and inevitable response, reference was made to 'world experience', the examples of the United States, Natal and Transvaal being cited (1967: 208-9). Thus, the hostile reaction of Australians was interpreted not as racism but as an inherent preference of the Australian (or 'white') 'race' to ensure its survival. To allow members of different 'races' to live in Australia would therefore stimulate the expression of this 'primary instinct': the presence of the racialised Other was thereby represented as the problem, the solution to which, logically, was to prevent their settlement. Hence, Willard argued that, because it is 'natural' that people belonging to supposedly different 'races' will wish to sustain their distinct and separate communities, the boundary of inclusion/exclusion that defined the imagined community of Australia was necessarily drawn by reference to 'race'. This argument advanced in the 1920s is very similar to that articulated in Britain in the 1980s and suggests that what has been defined as the new racism has a longer pedigree than the concept suggests.

It is certainly the case that sections of the Australian working class believed that their income would be reduced by an increasing number of Asian workers who entered unfree relations of production and who worked for lower wages (Dallas 1955: 49, 52). And there was justification for this interpretation where employers legitimated their recruitment by arguing that the cost was low when compared with those of recruiting and retaining European labour (for example, de Lepervanche 1984: 38). But the arguments against the Asian and Pacific island presence in the Australian colonies were also political in nature. In the case of the agitation against indentured Pacific island labour in Queensland, liberal-minded politicians made common cause with working class opposition, claiming that the use of such a source of labour facilitated the development of large landed estates and absenteeism, created contempt for certain kinds of manual labour and obstructed the development of democratic institutions (Willard 1967: 161, Connell and Irving 1980: 122). Thus the fact that Pacific island labourers were enmeshed in unfree relations of production was signified as a means of formulating a sense of common community by defining them as the Other for economic and political reasons.

But the significance of economic and political relations cannot be divorced from the ideological context in which the demand for exclusion was articulated. The European (predominantly British) settlers of the nineteenth century brought with them a discourse of 'race' and the agitation against the recruitment and employment of Indians, Chinese, and Pacific islanders took a racist form in so far as these populations were signified as distinct and inferior 'races' with undesirable secondary characteristics (see Davison 1985). The Labour movement was as much a leading force in the expression of this racism as sections of the emergent bourgeoisie (McQueen 1970: 50-5). Moreover, although the openly racist provisions of the legislation as originally drafted were dropped, the debate on the 1901 Act revealed that racism was a determinant motive in the formulation of the legislation. In the course of the debates, the alleged biological inferiority of the 'coloured races' was cited as a reason for their exclusion from Australia (Palfreeman 1972: 137) and Yarwood comments, 'Men [sic] in 1901 had seen little reason to doubt that the white races enjoyed an inherent superiority, which appeared to have been amply demonstrated by their conquests in Africa and Asia in the previous twenty years' (1964: 24). The use of racism as a form of representation was therefore an independent determinant which was nevertheless dependent upon the existence of material conflicts which required interpretation and negotiation. In this sense, racism was a practically adequate ideology.

Thus, in late nineteenth century Australia, a sense of imagined community was formulated in the light of the experience of the European settlers in dealing with, *inter alia*, Aboriginal resistance to their presence and conflicts provoked by recruiting labour from the South Pacific and parts of Asia. The boundary that was to determine the membership of the imagined community was drawn using the idea of 'race' as a criterion of inclusion/exclusion. On the basis of this racialisation of the potential imagined community, additional criteria were employed to establish a hierarchy of 'races', with the consequence that the parameters of Australian nationalism and the criterion of admission to the Australian nation state were shaped in part by racism. Hence, the 'inferior races' were excluded in the interests of sustaining a supra-class entity that had the potential to sustain a sense of common identity, a common identity grounded in a particular combination of cultural and biological homogeneity. By these means, those groups whose labour power had been appropriated under relations of unfreedom to sustain economic development were subsequently excluded from membership of the imagined community of a 'White Australia'.

CONCLUSION

In confronting the problem of the meaning of the concept of racism in the context of a process of conceptual inflation, I have sought a solution by trying to situate it in a set of interrelated concepts. Thus, rather than assent to the ever-broadening concept of racism, I have argued that it should be more narrowly defined as an ideology if it is to be of serious analytical value. My emphasis upon signification and representation therefore associates my argument with the rather different traditions outlined in chapter 2 of, on the one hand, Weberian theorists such as Rex and, on the other, Marxist cultural studies theorists such as Hall who nevertheless share the view that the concept of racism refers to a specific form of ideology. Consequently, my interest is in the production and reproduction of meanings, a focus that leads to a particular emphasis upon systems of communication in order to understand the reproduction of racism (for example, Hartmann and Husband 1974, Hall *et al*. 1978, van Dijk 1984, Murray 1986, Searle 1987, Gordon 1987).

But in deflating the definition, I have recognised the empirical significance of many of the historical transformations that have occurred and which have stimulated this conceptual inflation. Most significantly, although explicit expressions of a belief in the existence of a hierarchy of biologically distinct 'races' are much less widely articulated, especially in the formal public arena, a discourse of 'race' continues, along with a signification of somatic features and an attribution of negatively evaluated characteristics to groups so defined. I have argued that such a discourse should be defined as racism. But I have also argued that the expression of racism is an integral component of a wider, historical process of racialisation which is interlinked with exclusionary practices and with the expression of other forms of exclusionary ideology. In a social context structured by historical change and, in a post-colonial and post-Fascist era, by a desire to obscure intentionality, our conceptual framework warrants a greater degree of complexity and sophistication than is allowed by those who employ the concept of racism in a loose or undefined manner.

4

Class relations

INTRODUCTION

I have discussed racialisation and racism as representational phenomena in the previous chapter. However, as the discussion of the ideological articulation between nationalism and racism (illustrated by the example of late nineteenth century Australia) suggested, it is not possible to divorce their effectivity from the wider context of economic and political relations. In this chapter, I confront the interrelation between racialisation and racism and the historical development of capitalism as a mode of production within a developing world economic system. The effectivity of racialisation and racism is to be measured less in their simple presence or absence than in their articulation within the totality of relations within historically specific social formations. I set about this task against the background of a history of economistic analysis where there is a strong tendency to present racism as 'functional' to capitalist development in general, and to the bourgeoisie in particular (for example, Cox 1970: 322, Nikolinakos 1973: 367, Castles and Kosack 1972: 16, Wallerstein 1983: 78-80), a trend that I have criticised elsewhere (Miles 1982: 81-7, 1986).

I prefer to regard racialisation and racism as historically specific and necessarily contradictory phenomena. I mean a number of interconnected things by this. Racism has not only appeared in a number of different forms but also has a varying articulation with economic and political relations in capitalist and non-capitalist social formations. The evidence in chapter 1 demonstrates that racialisation and racism are not exclusive 'products' of capitalism but have origins in European societies prior to the development of the capitalist mode of production and have a history of expression within social formations dominated by non-capitalist modes of production in articulation with the capitalist mode. In other words, it is an ideology with conditions of existence which are, at least in part, independent of the interests of the bourgeoisie, a class specific to the capitalist mode of production, and therefore specific to a certain period of history.

Moreover, to define racism as functional to capitalism is to presuppose the nature and outcome of its articulation with economic and political relations, and with other ideologies. Such a definition mistakenly assumes that a homogeneous ruling class inevitably and necessarily derives economic and/or political advantages from its expression. The use of racism to limit the size of the labour market is not necessarily in the interests of those employers experiencing a labour shortage, while racism and exclusionary practices that result in civil disturbance will not necessarily be welcomed by capitalists whose business activity has been disrupted as a result, or by the state that has to increase expenditure to maintain social order.

Hence, I prefer to analyse racism as a necessarily contradictory phenomenon. The expression of racism, and the subsequent structuring of political and economic relations, will have a variety of temporally specific consequences for all of those implicated in the process, and whether or not they are advantageous will depend upon class position and conjuncture. Racism is therefore a contradictory phenomenon because what is 'functional' for one set of class interests can be 'dysfunctional' for another set of such interests, and because the conditions that sustain its (for one class, or class fraction) advantageous expression are rarely permanent, and changed circumstances may clash with the continued expression of racism. It follows that the effectivity of racism is therefore historically specific and hence knowable only as a result of historical analysis rather than as a result of abstract theorising. The objective of this chapter is to illustrate and elaborate these claims.

CAPITALISM, COLONIALISM AND UNFREE LABOUR

As was observed in chapter 1, European colonialism assumed a number of different developmental patterns. But what they all had in common from the mid-seventeenth century until the early twentieth century was a process whereby Europeans occupied and settled on land in other parts of the world, and subsequently, if not immediately, organised the production of use values as commodities for exchange on the world market. European occupation often, although not exclusively, led to the use of force, while the latter usually required either the diversion of the use values produced within an extant mode of production or the transformation of an extant mode of production in order to create a supply of labour for the system of production initiated by the European settlers.

Thus, from the mid-seventeenth century onwards, European represent-ations of the Other were generated and reproduced in the course of a history of contact between different populations enmeshed in specific forces and relations of production and expressing distinct cultural values. These representations actively structured, rather than simply legitimated, the transformation of existing modes of production, with the result that they became a historical condition for the reproduction of either the modifed, extant modes of production, or the new modes of production created in the colonial context. That is, these discourses became a 'relation of production', an ideological component of the totality of relations that constituted not only a system of production in the narrow sense but a whole way of living (cf. Sayer 1987: 63-77).

Where modes of production were created anew in the colonial context, they rarely took the form that was emergent in Europe, that which was based on the generalisation of commodity production and therefore the commodification of labour power. The development of wage labour as a relation of production was dependent on, *inter alia*, divorcing previous agricultural producers from the land, requiring them to seek a buyer for their labour power, and in sufficient numbers to ensure that there was competition between them to regulate the price that they could command. This process of 'primary accumulation' did not occur in the same manner in the colonial context for a variety of reasons, and the relations of production that did emerge were characterised to a greater or lesser degree by forms of direct physical and legal-political compulsion, that is, by forms of unfree labour and hence by specific forms of class relations (cf. Miles 1987a, Kolchin 1987).

From the eighteenth to the early twentieth centuries, European colonisation was motivated to varying degrees by military/strategic and economic motives, but even where the former dominated, economic interests subsequently came to the fore in order to generate revenue to sustain the colonisation. The successful development of a system of production presumed that a number of conditions could be satisfied. It was necessary to identify some mineral or agricultural item which could be obtained or produced and which could become a commodity for sale on the world market. And in order to produce this commodity, access to land and the provision of a labour supply had to be organised. The latter entailed not only the identification of people who would provide labour power but also the establishment of the conditions under which that population would actually make labour power available (that is, establishing the relations of production) and suppressing their resistance to such attempts. Both, in turn, presumed the prior possession or provision of a sum of money with which to effect this organisation. The argument that follows is concerned largely with the procedures by which access to land and labour power was gained.

The particular procedures employed were determined in part by whether or not the region of settlement was already occupied, and by the nature of not only the mode of production, but the totality of economic, political and ideological relations governing the lives of the already resident population.

Where the region was unoccupied or only sparsely populated, gaining access to land was largely unproblematic, at least initially, although recruiting a labour force was made correspondingly more difficult and could only be effected by migration and/or settlement from some other region. Where the land was occupied, that population was potentially available to provide labour power, but its access to land was an obstacle to colonial settlement and the organisation of production. In the example that I wish to consider here, that of Kenya, the latter conditions prevailed.

This organisation of production in colonial Kenya was a material process sustained and effected by racialisation and the expression of racism. The European colonisers and the African indigenous populations met each other as human beings already organised into classes and, at least as far as the former were concerned, against the background of a long history of 'knowing' the African through a variety of written and oral sources (as we have already seen) and, in the case of some colonisers, previous experience of having met and lived amongst Africans. They came to Africa, therefore, with a representation of the African as Other, a representation that was logically related to the rationale that they formulated to explain their presence and settlement, the rationale of civilising people who were at a less advanced stage of development (Thornton 1965: 158). It was on the basis of the presuppositions about the African as an inferior human being that the process of primary accumulation was carried through, with the result that the economic relations of production that were established had a particular ideological content.

The British colonisers arrived in Kenya with a discourse of 'race'. As we have seen in chapter 1, this was a ranking that placed the African at the bottom of a scale of 'civilisation' and gave the European colonisers a specific responsibility. Thus, an employee of the Imperial British East Africa Company claimed, 'the ability to administer native races is one of the heritages of our race in which we may have just pride' (cited in Sorrenson 1968: 242, also Bennett 1965: 314). In the mid-1920s, at a time when the colonial ruling class was confident that its strategy would succeed, Sir Robert Coryndon, Governor of Kenya, stated

> The 'settlers' should not now be regarded as merely a turbulent
> wayward colony of wayward children, but a group of strong men
> [*sic*] very determined to maintain their duty to their race and colour,
> very sensible of responsibilities to the native population, and always
> striving upwards. (cited in Brett 1973: 183)

In carrying out that responsibility, it was considered necessary to take account of the implications of this difference of 'race' because it was believed to set biological limits to what might be achieved by the European male presence (for example, Lugard 1929: 64, 193ff). Not for the first time was the discourse of colonialism one which defined it as an exclusively masculine project.

The majority of the African population was, in the early twentieth century, widely regarded by Europeans as being of the 'negro race'. This 'race' was described as follows by one British colonial administrator:

> In colour they are very black, with woolly hair growing in little tufts on the scalp, and with practically none on the face ... In character and temperament the typical African of this race-type is a happy, thriftless, excitable person, lacking in self-control, discipline, and foresight, naturally courageous, and naturally courteous and polite, full of personal vanity, with little sense of veracity, fond of music, and 'loving weapons as an oriental loves jewelry' ... The African negro is not naturally cruel, though his own insensibility to pain, and his disregard for life - whether his own or another's - cause him to appear callous to suffering. (Lugard 1929: 68-9)

He summarised his construction of the African as Other as: 'In brief, the virtues and the defects of this race-type are those of attractive children, whose confidence when once it has been won is given ungrudgingly as to an older and wiser superior, without question and without envy' (1929: 70).

For those who also believed in social Darwinism, 'civilising the natives' was considered to have dire consequences which they accepted without equivocation. Sir Charles Elliot, who was one of the early Commissioners of the East African Protectorate, wrote in a memorandum to the Foreign Office in London, in April 1904,

> Your Lordship has opened this Protectorate to white immigration and colonisation, and I think it well that in confidential correspondence at least, we should face the undoubted issue – viz., that the white mates black in a very few moves ... There can be no doubt that the Masai and many other tribes must go under. It is a prospect which I view with equanimity and a clear conscience ... [Masaidom] is a beastly, bloody system founded on raiding and immorality. (Bennett 1965: 270-1)

Others believed that the 'civilising' process was less a process of genocide, and more a matter of patient acceptance of slow change. An official government memorandum on 'native policy' stated

In dealing with African savage tribes we are dealing with a people at the genesis of things ... and we cannot expect to lift them in a few years from this present state to that of a highly civilised people ... The evolution of races must necessarily take centuries to accomplish satisfactorily. (cited in Sorrenson 1968: 227)

Others were less patient. A settler protest against the proposal for a common electoral roll and an equal franchise stated the belief that the theory of waiting 'till the backward races (whom the Report itself describes as twenty centuries behind the Europeans) have reached their standard is an impossible proposition that no virile and governing race could be expected to acquiesce in' (cited in Bennett 1965: 310).

The idea of 'race' as a biological reality was given legal status in treaties and legislation. The agreement that removed the Masai from the Rift Valley in the East African Protectorate and established the Masai reserve required their representatives to confirm that they were 'fully satisfied that the proposals for our removal to definite and final reserves are for the undoubted good of our race' (Sorrenson 1968: 195) while the 1915 Crown Lands Ordinance defined 'race' as 'persons of European, Asiatic or African origin as the case may be' (Sorrenson 1968: 174, see also 141). The settlers therefore racialised the African populations that they came to 'civilise' and they necessarily racialised themselves as the agents of 'civilisation'. Indeed, this was a universal process in so far as the population of the whole world was racialised, and racism created a hierarchy of suitability amongst the 'races'.

Thus, when the Colonial Secretary in London suggested that the infant colony be opened to Jewish refugees from Eastern Europe, the arguments of the early settlers opposing this were openly racist (Mungeam 1966: 104, Sorrenson 1968: 38-9). But the crucial practical issue for the settlers was the manner in which the 'civilisation' of the savage and backward African 'race' might be achieved. The settlers' primary solution was that the African should provide labour power for the European who had gained access to the land but who had little or no intention to labour on it. In the view of one settler who spoke for the majority, the 'white man' was 'the master race and ... the black men must forever remain cheap labour and slaves' (cited in Sorrenson 1968: 238). This racism was a class ideology. It was a representation of a group of people who had gained access to the means of production with the objective of making others work for them.

This was a discourse which, by ranking people on a supposed scale of natural worth and capacity, invented a biological hierarchy of the world's population which thereby fitted certain groups for certain positions in the relations of production. Thus, the 'white race' was destined not only to rule politically, but also to organise and direct production, and the African 'race' was destined to provide it with labour power in order that a surplus from agricultural commodity production might be realised. Thus, racism was a central dimension of the creation of a labour force for a landowning class. Racism was not simply a legitimation of class exploitation (although it was that) but, more important, it constructed the social world in a way that identified a certain population as a labouring class. The problem that remained was to organise the social world in such a way that forced that population into its 'natural' class position: in other words, reality had to be brought into line with that representation in order to ensure the material objective of production.

In order to understand how that was achieved, it is necessary to consider the material circumstances of the African populations at the time of European settlement. Within East Africa, and with the exception of the coastal strip, the land was occupied by a number of spatially and culturally distinct populations engaged largely in subsistence production (Sorrenson 1968: 28, Brett 1973: 168, Tignor 1976: 3-4, 14). The latter was often, although not exclusively, dependent upon migration from one location to another as grazing for livestock was exhausted. The British colonisers of the late nineteenth century (some of whom came via the South African colonies and were accompanied by settlers of Dutch origin) therefore minimally had to convince or force these populations to give up land to permit their own settlement, and to provide them with labour power when these African populations were already well able to satisfy their own material wants. Collectively, the measures by which these objectives were achieved established a form of commodity production based on unfree labour alongside the reproduction of subsistence production, and therefore a particular configuration of classes.

Gaining access to land was one of the first problems confronted by the European colonisers, and one that required the use of force in order to establish the initial settlement (Low 1965: 31, Tignor 1976: 15). Once residence had been established, the settlers had then to gain control over sufficient land to permit the development of agricultural commodity production. This led to a conflict of interests with the African populations who used the land for subsistence production as well as with the population of Indian origin which had been long present in East Africa as merchants and traders. The central strategy employed by the settlers, and effected by the colonial state, was to establish exclusive European access to land in areas considered suitable climatically for European occupation and agricultural production (the 'White Highlands', as they became known), to dispossess the Africans resident in these areas and to create African reserves where the indigenous populations could reproduce themselves in areas adjacent to those occupied by European landowners (Tignor 1976: 30-2). Indians, too, were excluded from owning or renting land in the Highlands and were subject to restrictions on where they might live in the towns (Sorrenson 1965: 680-2, 1968: 159-75). These conflicting interests ensured an ongoing process of resistance and accommodation on the part of the African and Indian populations to European colonisation.

The creation of reserves was not originally intended by the settlers (Sorrenson 1965: 683) and was achieved somewhat haphazardly by two means, both of which were facilitated by the creation of African chiefs by the dominant colonial class. Few African populations in Kenya had individual chiefs but it did not prove too difficult to find individuals willing to fulfil this role when they were usually able to accumulate land and livestock as a result of so doing (Mungeam 1966: 129-30, Tignor 1976: 42, 49, Sender and Smith 1986: 42-3). The first mechanism was that, under the terms of the East Africa (Lands) Order in Council (1901) and the Crown Lands Ordinance (1902), land that was considered by the settlers to be unoccupied and unexploited by Africans was defined as 'waste' land and was then made available to European settlers by means of sale or leasehold, thereby establishing private property relations (Wrigley 1965: 227-8, Sorrenson 1965: 675-7, 682). From the point of view of the African populations, whose mode of production entailed the periodic movement from one location to another rather than permanent occupation of an area, this entailed setting limits on their previous migratory patterns. In other words, what for the European settlers was 'waste' land was for the Africans land always potentially available for temporary production and residence.

The second need was to 'negotiate' with African populations to define the spatial boundaries within which they would be bound to live, and in the special case of the Masai, for their removal to other locations under the terms of a treaty to free the land for European occupation (Sorrenson 1968: 182-9, 210-25). This process began in the very early years of the twentieth century (Mungeam 1966: 202-4), but it was not until the Crown Land Ordinance (1915) that the Governor of the colony was given the power to proclaim the creation of reserves and so most were not formally constituted until 1926 (Sorrenson 1965: 683, Tignor 1976: 32). Moreover, their boundaries were subject to subsequent revision in order to release more land for European settlement and it was only as a result of the enquiry of the Kenya Land Commission (appointed in 1932) that the boundaries were finally established (Wrigley 1965: 259-60, Sorrenson 1965: 687-89).

For the European settlers, the establishment of reserves by the colonial state, with support from London, was central to establishing control over land, but by itself it did not permit the constitution of agricultural commodity production. Although initial settler plots were relatively small (Wrigley 1965:

219), they came to exceed 5,000 acres in some cases and these were certainly too large to be farmed by a single family (Low 1965: 51). Thus, not only was land necessary but so were human beings to provide labour power. And the creation of reserves did not immediately make this provision because they appeared to have been established to permit the 'natives' to maintain their 'traditional' mode of life. Certainly, by allowing the Africans to retain direct access to land as the most important means of production, the creation of reserves in themselves did not force them into working for the European settlers. Indeed, in maintaining the material premise for African peasant production, that is, growing crops for the market, the reserves actually made it less likely that the Africans would also work for the European landowners (Stichter 1982: 44-5).

Various strategies were employed in order to procure African labour power, and as cheaply as possible, and all depended upon the intervention of the colonial state. Hence, the 'natural' role of the African 'race' to provide cheap labour power could only be achieved by human intervention. One method was the use of direct or indirect compulsion. This was widely used by the colonial state to construct the infrastructure of colonisation and to establish the conditions for agricultural commodity production. Forced labour was a development of African communal (unpaid) labour which was intended to produce collective benefits for the population from which the labourers were drawn and which was used for path-making and bush-clearing. The colonial state at district level modified this system, using the new 'chiefs' as intermediaries, to provide labourers for local road-building, the construction of 'public' buildings and for porterage. It also directed some communal labour on to farms (Tignor 1976: 43). After 1918, this system was further modified by the Native Authority Amendment Ordinance 1920, to the point that compulsion became dominant and explicit. The colonial state would demand of a local chief that a specified number of fit men be recruited for a certain period to construct roads, railways, and docks away from the men's place of residence, and in return for a small cash wage which was lower than that paid to voluntary labourers. Those nominated by the chief faced a variety of sanctions if they refused. Often, those recruited were required to work for private employers engaged in contracted tasks from the colonial state (Wrigley 1965: 231, 237, Clayton and Savage 1974: xvi-xvii, 29, 44, 134-9).

A second strategy was the 'squatter system' whereby African communities were encouraged to live on European-owned land and were expected to provide a certain amount of labour power during a year, in return for which they received the right to use a certain area of land in order to produce their means of subsistence (see Wrigley 1965: 231-2, Bennett 1965: 277). This was similar to the system of labour tenancy which had been established in South Africa (de Kiewiet 1941: 203) and, by the 1920s, was the relationship by which landowners obtained the largest proportion of labourers (Clayton and Savage 1974: 128). Within the terms of the Masters and Servants Ordinance 1906, employers could hire labourers on an annual contract. Those hired were required to work for the employer for a minimum of three months, in return for which they received free of rent an acre of land per head and a very small wage (Sorrenson 1968: 150, Clayton and Savage 1974: 32).

The 'squatter system' was modified by the Resident Natives Ordinance 1918 (Tignor 1976: 164), in response to an increasing tendency for Africans to pay cash for the use of land rather than provide labour power (as a result of which a class of tenant farmers began to emerge). This Ordinance stipulated that access to land could only be exchanged for labour power, and that this had to be provided for a minimum of 180 days (Clayton and Savage 1974: 128-31, Brett 1973: 171-2). This relation of production approximated serfdom but as agricultural production expanded, it became increasingly problematic for the landowner by virtue of the quantity of land occupied by Africans, and by the end of the following decade it was in decline and being replaced by a system of wage labour (Wrigley 1965: 257).

The third strategy was to 'induce' Africans 'voluntarily' to enter the emergent labour market where they would sell their labour power for a wage. 'Inducement' took two main forms. The first was taxation which became a central factor in the early 1920s (Tignor 1976: 183). By requiring Africans to pay a tax in cash to the colonial state, certain sections of the African population were thereby required to seek a means of obtaining a cash income which was at least sufficient to pay the tax. A hut tax was first introduced in 1901, although the original motivation was to raise revenue to cover the costs of colonial intervention and administration (Low 1965: 23). But by 1908 landowners were demanding that the hut tax be increased and a poll tax introduced, to be paid by all those not paying the former, in order to increase the supply of African labour power. In response, the colonial state introduced a poll tax in 1910 (Sorrenson 1968: 151, 155). The rates of taxation were increased in 1920 in a further attempt to effect the same outcome, although this proved a short term initiative because of African resistance to the increase (Brett 1973: 188, Clayton and Savage 1974: 143-6).

The second form of 'inducement' was the state's 'encouragement' of Africans to make their labour power available to landowners. This inducement was often direct but was usually mediated by the 'chiefs' who served in effect as colonial officials, especially during the early phase of colonisation (Tignor 1976: 53, 105, 182). But when evidence of such encouragement became public during the first decade of the twentieth century, there was conflict with the Colonial Office in London (Wrigley 1965: 231). The same sequence of events occurred after the First World War. In 1919 and 1920 the colonial state published circulars which stated the government's wish that Africans should provide labour power and which instructed its District Officers to use all lawful means to encourage the provision of labour power, and to press local chiefs and elders to do the same. In response to widespread criticism, these circulars were initially legitimated by Parliament in London as being in the 'real interests' of Africans because they were intended to eliminate 'idleness and vice' from the African way of life (although subsequently the policy was modified in 1921). This legitimation therefore reconciled the imperial, paternalistic mission of civilising the 'inferior races' with the task of providing a labour force for the 'superior, master race' (Brett 1973: 188-9, Clayton and Savage 1974: 32-41, 110-17, Tignor 1976: 173).

In combination with the establishment of the reserves, these two forms of inducement led to the creation of a migrant labour system within Kenya (Stichter 1982) which became firmly established during the 1920s, the decade which witnessed the major expansion of agricultural commodity production (of coffee, sisal, maize, and later, tea), organised by European landowners, for exchange on the world market (Wrigley 1965: 235, Brett 1973: 176, Tignor, 1976: 145). Throughout this decade, there was an increase in labour migration that coincided with a decline in forms of compulsory recruitment and of African peasant production. The latter was actively discouraged by the colonial state. For example, in the mid-1920s, in response to demands from European landowners involved in coffee production, the colonial state ruled that licences which permitted the growing of coffee should not be issued to Africans (Wrigley 1965: 245-6, Brett 1973: 208-11). Because there were few economies of scale to be achieved in growing coffee, the African peasant producer could compete successfully with the European landowner, and the latter therefore sought a political method of preventing competition. The motivation for the objection was less the fact that the African peasant producer might undercut the cost of European production and more to do with the implications of successful cash crop production for the labour supply (Tignor 1976: 292). As one European landowner put it (cited in Wrigley 1965: 246),

> it stands to reason that the more prosperous and contented is the population of a reserve, the less the need or inclination of the young men of the tribe to go out into the field. From the farmers' point of view the ideal reserve is a recruiting-ground for labour, a place from which the able-bodied go out to work, returning occasionally to rest and to beget the next generation of labours.

Hence, it was necessary for the colonial state to act to make the reserves incapable of producing sufficient for subsistence. Consequently, the reserves became less locations for the reproduction of the 'traditional' African way of life and more reservoirs of labour from which the European landowners could recruit when necessary. The decline in African peasant production was therefore a major factor in creating a migrant labour force because it meant that some other means of earning a cash income had to be found in order to pay the hut and poll taxes. Thus, the 'voluntary' search by an increasing proportion of African men for a purchaser for their labour power in the 'White Highlands' was grounded in socially constituted conditions of economic compulsion. These conditions were overdetermined during the 1920s when the spatially limited reserves began to be unable to produce enough to sustain the increasing African population (Stichter 1982: 30-89).

I have described here the forms of social intervention of a colonising class, supported by the state, intended to establish commodity production in a spatial location where the existing population reproduced itself in the absence of commodity production and money as a medium of exchange. The creation of this new mode of production entailed the reorganisation and subordination of that subsistence mode of production. This process of creating a section of the population partially or wholly freed of the means of production in order to compel the sale of labour power for a wage (that is, the process of creating a proletariat which is a central dimension of 'primary accumulation') is a universal feature of the transition to a capitalist mode of production, and necessarily depends upon various forms of compulsion. But, as Marx pointed out, it always takes a historically specific form (1976: 876).

The process of primary accumulation is often analysed primarily as a transformation of economic relations, and effected by the intervention of the state. But the process of transformation in Kenya (and elsewhere in Africa and the colonised world: see Sender and Smith 1986) was effected not only by political intervention (the role of the colonial state being central) but was also decisively shaped by racialisation and racism. The process of economic transformation was represented by the European invaders as an interaction between 'races', and the process of transition was effected by means of the racialisation of both the emergent landowning class and the partially dispossessed African. Hence, the people who were identified as the source of the labour power that the landowners would exploit as a class were constructed in thought by the landowners as an inferior 'race'. In other words, the socially determined process of class formation was racialised.

The classes so formed were therefore simultaneously universal and specific. They were universal in the sense that there are many other historical instances of primary accumulation in the course of which a class has established a partial or complete monopoly over the means of production, and as a result of which a class of wage labourers has been created. But they were specific in the sense that the process of class formation was shaped by racialisation: the creation of the partially dispossessed labouring class was not only motivated by racism but was effected through the institutionalisation of that racism in a system of racialised segregation, by which the different 'races' were allocated not only to different economic roles but also to different spatial locations. Economic and political relations were thereby socially constructed in accordance with the ideology of racism.

Again, there is a universal dimension to this process of spatial segregation in so far as every ruling class usually organises its life in a distinct spatial location, separated from the lives of those whose labour power is exploited. The specificity lies in the conscious and strategic institutionalisation of a particular representational construction, that is, racism. The ideology of racism was used not only to select certain people to fill certain positions in the structure of class relations but class relations were themselves structured in a particular manner to create a large proportion of Africans as suppliers of cheap labour power. The proletarian, or semi-proletarian, class position of the African was represented in thought as the appropriate position for a population at a different stage of human development, for a different (and inferior) kind of human being. To conclude, in this historically specific instance of primary accumulation, the labouring class was created by a dialectic between a process of material (but partial) dispossession of the means of production and a process of racialisation. Consequently, racism became a relation of production because it was an ideology which shaped decisively the formation and reproduction of the relation between exploiter and exploited: it was one of those representational elements which became historically conducive to the constitution and reproduction of a system of commodity production.

CAPITALISM, REPRODUCTION AND NATIONALISM

In the previous section, I was concerned with the historical significance of racialisation in the process of primary accumulation, the process by which the capitalist mode of production is constituted. In this and the following section, I argue that the process of racialisation and the expression of racism have become, under certain historical circumstances, central to two dimensions of the reproduction of the capitalist mode of production. The first concerns the role of the state in maintaining the conditions for the reproduction of the capitalist mode of production within any historically specific nation state, one aspect of which is the generation and reconstruction of a sense of 'imagined community'. The second concerns the processes by which people are allocated to the various sites of class relations, these sites being structurally determined by the historically specific articulation of modes of production within any particular nation state. Both of these processes are essential to the reproduction of the capitalist mode of production. Racialisation and racism may be therefore historically specific mechanisms by which these processes may be effected, and in their absence other representational forms will necessarily be present.

Concerning the first instance, it is necessary to begin by commenting on the interrelationship between capitalism and the nation state. The development of the capitalist mode of production in Europe has been synonymous with the development of the nation state. That is to say, a certain form of productive activity premised upon generalised commodity production and the dialectical interdependence between the classes of capitalist and wage labourer, has emerged within the context of a certain type of politico-spatial structure. Indeed, the spatial division of the world, and the formation of some form of centralised political authority claiming sovereignty within each space, was the context for the emergence of the capitalist mode of production and not a product of it (see Corrigan and Sayer 1986). Thus, capitalism did not suddenly emerge everywhere but did so first in England, in a territorial unit that had been consolidated by the activity of a feudal state and a feudal ruling class. It is for this reason that the debate about the transition from feudalism to capitalism (for example, Hilton *et al.* 1978; Holton 1985) has been, in part, about why capitalism developed first in England.

Both the capitalist mode of production and the nation state, in their historically specific instances, are socially constructed by human beings. The emergence of capitalism depended upon active processes of material dispossession and concentration of wealth in order to create a class of people without access to the means of production who were therefore obliged to exchange their labour power for a wage, and a class which largely monopolised the means of production which sought to purchase labour power to combine with those means of production (see Miles 1987a: 20-4). And nation-state formation has often also involved the use of force, as well as negotiation, to include culturally distinct populations within an expanding territorial boundary and the active creation of myths of historical origin and tradition to justify their inclusion (for example, Hobsbawm 1983). This latter process is more recent than the former and was only justified by an ideology of nationalism (which claimed that *inter alia* 'nations' were naturally occurring populations each with a distinct cultural profile) from the late eighteenth century (Kedourie 1985: 9-19). In other words, historically, a number of nation states have been constituted in the absence of nationalism (Seton-Watson 1977: 6).

The state has been, and remains, central to the creation and reproduction of the capitalist mode of production and the nation. Indeed, these processes presuppose the existence of the state. The process of dispossession and concentration has been usually effected by some combination of legal procedure and physical force while the expansion of the boundaries of the nation state to incorporate other populations has usually required compulsion. Moreover, once capitalism has been established, antagonistic class interests give rise to conflict that must be mediated, contained and suppressed. And, in a world divided into nation states, the existence of one may be threatened by the economic and political interests of the ruling class of another. Hence, the state effects strategies to protect and advance the interests of those who own capital located within its boundaries and to maintain its territorial space against physical invasion. The mediation of class conflict and the protection of the boundaries of the nation are tasks effected by the state which therefore include amongst its institutions a legal system, armed forces, and police.

Anderson (1983) has traced the connections between the rise of capitalism and the expression of nationalism as a representational form that purported to identify culturally and historically distinct populations, each with a 'natural right' to govern itself. The nationalist political project was therefore coupled with a representational project with the objective of constructing both a history and an emotional sense of shared distinctiveness which would, in turn, create a collective sense of Self defined dialectically by the presence of the Other. For Anderson, the crucial determinant in this project was the coincidence of the development of print-languages and the generalisation of commodity production, one instance of which was the book, which created the possibility of imagining a nation (1983: 41-9).

But language was simultaneously medium and message: not only was a difference of language used to create a sense of community of readers and speakers, but it also permitted the generation of explanations for differences of language which could legitimate an idea of a distinct nation. Historical writing assumed the responsibility for identifying the unique 'spirit' and characteristics of a nation, each instance of which was constructed as a real thing in itself, a living entity. This process of reification was accompanied by a search for the origin of each nation (Barzun 1938: 40-1). And during the nineteenth century, when the process of capitalist development and a conscious strategy of nation-state formation within Europe was at its most vigorous, many (but certainly not all) advocates of nationalism drew upon scientific racism in order to identify these supposedly distinct, natural collectivities. As I have argued elsewhere, racism was especially appropriate to this task because it suggested that the natural differences between 'nations' were grounded in biology and this constituted perhaps the most solid defence of the idea of historical inevitability that is central to the nationalist doctrine (Miles 1987c: 41, see also Mosse 1978: 50, 94).

We have already seen that the discourse of 'race' used by Europeans to define an Other beyond the boundary of Europe as biologically inferior was first used by certain political forces within Europe to differentiate populations, to constitute Self and Other dialectically, as separate nations. However, a classification of 'races' that identified Caucasian, Negro, and Mongoloid as the main categories, although it clearly served to distance Europeans, represented collectively as Caucasians, from so-called Negro and Mongoloid 'races', had limited utility by itself in distinguishing between different populations within Europe. But this tripartite classification of 'races' was not the only classification available, as was demonstrated in chapter 1. When attention turned specifically to Europe, divisions were hypothesised between, for example, Nordic (or Teutonic), Roman and Gallic (or Celtic) 'races' and between Aryan and Semitic 'races' (Barzun 1938: 28, 31-2, 135-49).

Anderson has argued that it was the systematic identification, classification and analysis of languages, and the subsequent concretisation of language in print as a commodity in the form of texts (books, magazines, pamphlets) for sale, that was 'central to the shaping of nineteenth-century European nationalisms' (1983: 69, also Seton-Watson 1977: 9). However, in many of these classifications, language was identified not only as the central signifier and therefore unifier of the imagined community, but also as the expression of 'race' (Barzun 1938: 135, Mosse 1978: 38-41). Language was represented as a difference in itself but, for some nationalists, it was also a sign of a more fundamental form of differentiation between European populations, a difference of biology. Even when it was argued that all current nations were composite populations, containing different mixtures of a number of 'races', it was also concluded that the proportion of the mix of superior and inferior 'races' determined the position of the 'nation' on the scale of superiority and inferiority. Indeed, for Gobineau, it was the inevitable mixing of inferior and superior 'races' that led to 'degeneration' and which therefore determined the course of historical development (see Mosse 1978: 51-5). This idea of 'degeneration' played a central role in the rise of the eugenics movement and in asserting Aryan superiority and Jewish inferiority in Germany (Mosse 1978: 82-8, for an example, see Günther 1970: 197-8, 267).

Taken together these two features permitted certain architects of the ideology of nationalism in any single country to claim that its population was superior in some way on the strength of claims that it contained a much larger proportion of, for example, Nordic or Aryan blood, or that a certain superior 'race' first emerged or inhabited its territorial space (for example, Barzun 1938: 144). Thus, while nationalists in Germany, France, and Britain all employed some version of the argument that the Teutonic or Anglo-Saxon 'race' had an inherent capacity and desire for democratic institutions and freedom, they each found some reason to claim that this inherent capacity was superior within the nation state which was the subject of their imagination (Mosse 1978: 48-9, 66-7, also Horsman 1976, 1981). The discourse of 'race' was employed therefore not only to ascribe negatively evaluated characteristics to, for example, Africans but also to create a positive sense of imagined community within Europe, in the course of which negatively evaluated characteristics were ascribed to other Europeans. In so doing, Europeans differentiated and racialised themselves in the course of effecting and rein-forcing national boundaries during the nineteenth century.

The Europeans engaged in the creation and mobilisation of nationalist sentiment in order to create nation states in the nineteenth century were largely members of the rising bourgeoisie, and they drew upon the ideas of an intelligensia (Nairn 1981: 96-103, 153-4). For this rising class, nationalism was a means to overthrow monarchic and aristocratic political domination (Kedourie 1985: 12-13) and to secure political control within a territorial unit that would permit the accumulation of capital on a scale to allow competition with units of capital located in extant nation states. In this sense, nationalism was rooted in the uneven development of capitalism. The nationalism of this rising class was therefore an ideology of unification (Hobsbawm 1977: 5), in the sense of not only creating a sense of community but also of establishing spatial boundaries within which the interrelated processes of capital accumulation and proletarianisation could occur. In the pursuit of these interests, the rising bourgeoisie had to mobilise politically those people whom it would subsequently subject to its economic and political domination and it could only do so by creating a sense of imagined community, of common interests. It had to represent those particularistic interests as the collective interests of the nation, and this was achieved by signifying whatever 'differentiae', as Nairn expresses it (1981: 340), that were available.

While accepting this argument which links nationalism with liberalism, it is mistaken to believe that all nineteenth century nationalisms were linked to political movements of democratic reform. If one does, it becomes impossible to explain the previously mentioned articulation of racism and nationalism which had more conservative implications. In the case of France, for example, once the emergent bourgeoisie had achieved its objective of sweeping away the old political order by a mobilisation of the emergent working class, it then had to defend the new order against the demands of sections of this class that found that individual political liberty did not mean the elimination of economic exploitation. Thus, after 1871, nationalism was reconstructed by a section of the dominant class in order to portray the nation state as the supreme political value which had to be defended against various forces of dissolution and corruption. These included not only socialists but Protestants and Jews (Seton-Watson 1977: 449). The discourse of 'race' was then used to identify an Other within the nation state in order to heighten the sense of imagined community and therefore consciousness of the role of this dominant class in protecting the nation state from disintegration.

The situation in Germany was different in so far as, unlike France, the objective of creating a nation state had, in the late nineteenth century, not been fully realised (Seton-Watson 1977: 89). In the early nineteenth century, this objective had been sought by means of an articulation between nationalism and liberalism but later in the century, a strong nationalist movement developed in Austria amongst a section of the rising bourgeois class; this represented Jewish involvement in commercial and professional activities as a brake on their own economic and political advancement. In arguing that the German ruling class contained men who had betrayed the nation by allowing an Other to seek and achieve economic and political domination, the discourse of 'race' played a key role. These arguments were to gain a new vitality following military defeat and the development of a sense of national humiliation after 1918, and became central to the rise of Fascism (Seton-Watson 1977: 98, 449).

In both these cases, therefore, the differentiae that were available to be signified could be grounded in the discourse of 'race'. Where such grounding occurred, the ideas of 'nation' and 'race' were not so much identical (Mosse 1978: 45) as mutual reflections, each highlighting and magnifying the other in the manner of an image in opposite, facing mirrors. Hence, racism was (and remains) an ideology which can simultaneously define positive qualities in Self as well as negative qualities in the Other and therefore, in such circumstances, it 'thinks in terms of historical destinies' in exactly the same manner as nationalism (cf. Anderson 1983: 136, Gilroy 1987: 44-5).

Seton-Watson puzzles over whether the French nationalism of the late nineteenth century can really be defined as such because it did not constitute a component part of a movement for political independence (1977: 449). The problem originates in limiting a definition of nationalism in this way. Once a nation state exists, and with capitalist interests intertwined politically in its constitution, the nationalist objective inevitably shifts from nation-state formation to that of guaranteeing the economic and political conditions which sustain the reproduction of the nation state. Thus, if the main nationalist project in Europe of the nineteenth century was the creation of a sense of imagined community, during the twentieth century it has increasingly become one of reproducing the sense of imagined community in a rapidly changing material context, a context that demonstrates that the relationship between the capitalist mode of production and the nation state is contradictory rather than functional.

Whilst specific capitalist and proletarian classes have an existence grounded in a particular nation state (as a result of which they always have a certain cultural character and profile), the movements of capital and labour have become increasingly international, with the result that the existence of national boundaries potentially constitute obstacles to their circulation. The process of circulation is dictated by the central dynamic of the capitalist mode of production, the accumulation of capital (Marx 1976: 762-801). The competitive nature of capitalist production results in ongoing processes of capital centralisation and concentration in particular, but also changing spatial locations, processes that in turn have implications for the size of the working population in those various locations. This process occurs within and (increasingly) across national boundaries, with the result that labour (along with capital) must be permitted to circulate within and (increasingly) across those national boundaries in order to fill particular economic sites.

The international circulation of labour power is, unlike the circulation of capital, simultaneously a spatial mobility of human beings: labour power is a capacity of human beings and cannot be divorced from their physical presence. But in a world of nation states, human beings express a totality of cultural attributes (for example, language, dress, diet), which are in part signs of their being constituted originally within a specific nation state, and possess a legal status and an identity as its citizens. Nationality may be compared with membership of a club which permits exclusive access to its facilities and services but simultaneously bars, at least formally, the holder from access to the facilities and services of all other clubs. Thus, access to any other club requires the permission of the officials. In a world of nation states, nationality is potentially a factor of international immobilisation, and mobility therefore becomes conditional upon states permitting the entry of 'aliens', or members of other clubs. But even where entry is granted, their distinct cultural profile has the potential to be signified as a measure of their membership of another.

A very particular contradiction has arisen from this set of historically constituted circumstances. Where the process of capital accumulation is obstructed by a shortage of labour power within the nation state, the state is faced with the possibility of permitting or organising the recruitment of labour from outside the nation state in order to effect its central role as the guarantor of the conditions for the reproduction of the capitalist mode of production. This requires the establishment of the legal conditions for the permanent or temporary entry of citizens of other nation states to fill vacant sites in the hierarchy of class relations. Throughout Western Europe (with the partial exception of Britain), from the late 1940s until the early 1970s, the state established a contract migrant worker system (Castles *et al*. 1984: 11-39) to resolve the problem of labour shortage by permitting the temporary entry of foreign nationals. However, because of conjunctural contradictions (Miles 1986), many of these temporary entrants became effectively permanent settlers (but, so far, rarely citizens), as did ex-colonial migrants who, by way of contrast, entered Western Europe as citizens of the colonial nation state. Both groups have been joined by a flow of migrants who have entered Western European nation states as political refugees (for example, Paludan, 1981).

But the ideology of nationalism purports to identify a naturally occurring population distinguished by a unique complex of cultural characteristics. This complex is considered to constitute the basis of a homogeneous community and hence to override any other form of differentiation, particularly that which arises from structurally determined class differences. The presence of these migrant populations, where they possess a range of characteristics distinct from those imagined to unify the indigenous population, therefore has the potential to be signified as instrusive, as a dislocation of community. Two issues arise. First, whether the potential is realised depends upon whether or not a process of signification is prompted. What matters is not difference *per se* but the identification of difference as significant, and this requires an investigation of the conditions under which processes of signification occur. Second, where signification does occur, and under specific historical circumstances, there exists the potential for an articulation between nationalism and racism.

The migrant presence has become the object of political debate within the various European nation states during the previous quarter of a century. The periodisation of this process varies, however, from one social formation to another: in Britain and Switzerland, for example, the migrant presence was problematised in the formal political arena by the mid-1960s, whereas in France, West Germany, and the Netherlands, a similar process did not occur until the 1970s. A further measure of the unevenness of this political development may be found in a comparative analysis of the rise of neo-Fascist political parties (Husbands 1982): in Britain, the National Front achieved political prominence and some limited success during the 1970s (see Walker 1977, Fielding 1981, Taylor 1982), while in France the identically named National Front became a significant political force in the 1980s (see Ogden, 1987).

The totality of this historical variation and specificity remind us that there is no simple correlation between representational and political processes on the one hand and economic processes on the other, for it demonstrates that the migrant presence was problematised within the political arena in some nation states before the development of the economic crisis of capitalism in the early 1970s. Thus, when seeking an explanation for the occurrence of the signification of the migrant presence, it cannot be explained simply or solely as an attempt by the ruling classes of Western Europe to recreate a sense of imagined community by defining an Other as an illegitimate presence in a period of crisis which, *inter alia*, has led to mass unemployment. The working class has the power to shape the political agenda outside periods of generalised crisis and in response to its own material circumstances and ideological conceptualisation as they have been perceived to have been influenced by the migrant presence. Thus, in certain European societies, the state has been forced to respond to demands 'from below', although often refracted through elected politicians, for the halting of immigration and the reduction in the size of the population of migrant origin (see DeLey 1983, Wihtol de Wenden 1987).

Identifying and explaining the ideological content of the process of signification is an equally complex task. Another measure of difference between the European nation states lies in the content of the representation of the nature of the problem, both officially and in everyday, common-sense terms (see Hammar 1985, Grillo 1985). In Holland, reference is usually made to *ethnic minorities* while, in France, it is to *immigrés* or to *étrangers*. In West Germany, the usual category is that of *Gastarbeiter* and in Switzerland it is *Fremdarbeiter* or *Arbeitskrafte*. In the case of Britain, the reference is to immigrants and the problem is usually defined as one of *race relations*. Finally, in Sweden, it is to *invanderer* that people usually refer. Hence, it is evident that the ideological content of the process of problematisation has varied from one social formation to another. It is therefore important to identify empirically the differences that are signified as important. It is certainly the case that the migrant presence permits a re-evaluation of Us on the part of sections of the indigenous population by their identification of the migrant as Other, but whether this is effected through the signification of cultural or biological characteristics, or some combination of both, cannot be determined in advance.

In the specific case of Britain, it is now clear that the problematisation of the migrant presence occurred through the signification of both biological and cultural characteristics, and that the working class played an active role in what was a process of racialisation. This process, and the related articulation of racism, was a significant political force before the onset of major economic crisis and it was a form of partially autonomous resistance from below in that it derived from the experience of competition for scarce resources and of localised economic decline (see Phizacklea and Miles 1980: 167-76). But, as we have already seen, the British state has been, too, an active agent of racialisation by, *inter alia*, passing exclusionary immigration legislation which has institutionalised racism and identifying young people of Caribbean origin as a threat to 'law and order'. In so doing, the economic and political consequences of the crisis of capital accumulation have been expressed in part through the idea of 'race', the object of which is the population of Caribbean and Asian origin: they have become an internal Other, represented in law, policing practices, politicians' speeches, and media reporting (as well as in the everyday discourse of the working class) as a problematic and undesirable presence, as not only a symptom but also a cause of crisis (Hall 1978, CCCS 1982: 9-46).

But this process of racialisation has articulated intimately with nationalism. The speeches of Enoch Powell during the late 1960s were widely condemned (and correctly) as expressing racism but their ideological content was as much, if not more, nationalist than racist. Powell was seeking to reconstruct a sense of Englishness in the context of economic decline and the exposure of the failures of Labourism as a political alternative to the Conservative Party. As Nairn has expressed it,

> It was more than a case of locating a new scapegoat: this scapegoat was to have the honour of restoring a popular content to English national self-consciousness, of stirring the English 'corporate imagination' into life once more, by providing a concrete way of focussing its vague but powerful sense of superiority. (Nairn 1981: 274)

As I have suggested elsewhere (1988a), Powell's discourse asserted that the coherence of the 'nation' (which he conceived as a homogenous cultural unit with a distinctive history) was subverted by the presence of a population of migrant origin which was actively reproducing its distinctiveness of both culture and 'race'. Consequently, the 'English people' were the true victims of migration and, as England was 'their' country, the only logical solution was to 'repatriate' the Other, the 'alien wedge', in order to restore historical and cultural unity (Powell 1969: 281-314, 1972: 189-212). For Powell, the issue was not whether or not people of Asian and Caribbean origin were inferior 'races', but rather one of reconstructing a positive sense of Englishness which he believed, combined with free market economics, would restore England's position in the world economy.

The representational content of this and many other similar political interventions is therefore classically nationalist but it is neatly lined, and therefore sustained, by racism. The articulation depends, in part, upon a simultaneous signification of cultural differentiae and somatic features: the Other is differentiated by skin colour as well as by clothing, diet, language and religion, for example. The presence of the Other is represented as problematic by virtue of, for example, its supposed use of the resources and facilities of 'our own people', its propensity to violence or its stimulation of the 'natural prejudice' of 'our own people' against those whose 'natural home' (or 'nation') is elsewhere in the world. The negation of the negation is represented as the catharsis of 'repatriation' (Miles and Phizacklea 1984, Miles 1988a).

It is a major failing of much British writing on the role of the state in the expression of racism that it generates an explanation which lacks comparative potential because it fails to acknowledge the ideological specificity of the British case. The language of 'inferior races' may have disappeared from the House of Commons (although not from the propaganda of extreme right-wing and Fascist groups: see Billig 1978: 124-90, Thurlow 1980) but in Britain the problematisation of the migrant presence has been consistently expressed in the discourse of 'race' and 'race relations'. This distinguishes the British situation from that of most other Western European countries. Nevertheless, although the specific discourse is different, throughout Western Europe the migrant presence is signified as problematic and has been used to highlight the existence of a boundary between Self and Other. In so far as that boundary is measured by reference to cultural differentiation alone, then it is an expression of nationalism. Whether or not it articulates with racism is a matter for comparative European research.

Thus, nationalism is a means to sustain a sense of commonality, particularly in periods of conflict and crisis within a nation state, and the state plays a central role in the articulation of this ideology in order to guarantee conditions for the reproduction of the capitalist mode of production. Hence, the state's admission of citizens of another nation state as a supplementary source of labour power admits a population which, at least potentially, may be identified as a threat to the imagined community. Thus, in post-1945 Western Europe, a contradiction is to be found in the activities of the state designed to effect its role: the state has simultaneously admitted to the nation state culturally distinct populations to resolve problems of labour shortage, the presence of whom may be cited as a disintegration of the imagined community, and has articulated an exclusionary nationalism to sustain that sense of imagined community. The fact that racism has also been articulated to the same end leads to the conclusion that theories of racism that seek explanation solely by reference to colonial strategies and experience have limited analytical power.

CAPITALISM, RACISM AND CLASS RELATIONS

I turn finally to another, equally central, aspect of the reproduction of the capitalist mode of production, that of the processes by which people are distributed to the various sites in the hierarchy of economic relations. This is an essential aspect of the reproduction of the capitalist mode of production because the accumulation process can be obstructed if, for example, there are insufficient numbers of people available to function as wage labourers. In order to consider the significance of racism in this process, I begin by outlining the position of people of Asian and Caribbean origin within British economic relations. The evidence demonstrates that these people occupied, in the mid-1980s, all the main economic sites in the relations of production determined by the capitalist mode of production (see also Miles 1982: 167-88, Field *et al*. 1981). I must add that position in economic relations does not constitute the totality of class position (Miles 1987b): I focus only on this dimension because of the constraints of space.

First, the majority of Asian and Caribbean men and women occupy a proletarian economic position: more than 65 per cent of Asian and Caribbean people of working age are economically active and in paid employment (Barber 1985: 469-70, Anon. 1987: 19-20). There are, however, significant differences according to sex and national origin. For example, 49 per cent of women are economically active compared with 83 per cent of men. Of those who are economically active, Pakistani and Bangladeshi men and women have the lowest proportion in paid employment (66 per cent and 60.4 per cent respectively) while East African men have the highest proportion (91.2 per cent). And, amongst the Caribbean population, 83.2 per cent of women are in paid employment, compared with 69 per cent of men. Of those who are economically active, 83 per cent of Caribbean men and 73 per cent of Asian men are in manual jobs, while the comparative figures for Caribbean and Asian women are 47 per cent and 52 per cent (Brown 1984: 305).

Second, Asian and Caribbean people are also a significant part of the relative surplus population: in 1984, amongst Asian and Caribbean people aged 16 years and over, 21.3 per cent of men and 19.1 per cent of women were unemployed (Barber 1985: 473-4). Again, there is considerable variation by sex and national origin. For men, the unemployment rate varies from 9 per cent in the case of East African Asians to 34 per cent in the case of Pakistanis/Bangladeshis, while for women it varies from 17 per cent for Caribbean women to 40 per cent in the case of Pakistanis/Bangladeshis. Additionally, Asian and Caribbean people aged between 16 and 34 years and born in Britain are more likely to be unemployed than those born outside Britain (Barber 1985: 47, Anon. 1983: 428).

Third, there is a small, but increasing, Asian and Caribbean *petite bourgeoisie*. The levels of self-employment are highest amongst people of Asian origin: 24.5 per cent of East African Asian men and 15.4 per cent of East African Asian women are self-employed, while for Indian and Pakistani/Bangladeshi men the proportions are 21.2 per cent and 16.6 per cent respectively, and for Indian and Pakistani/Bangladeshi women, the proportions are 9.9 per cent and 12.3 per cent respectively. Among those of Caribbean origin, 7.5 per cent of men and 1.5 per cent of women are self-employed (Anon. 1983: 429, Barber 1985: 475, Anon. 1987: 22). Fourth, there is a small Asian bourgeoisie (Wilson 1983, Werbner 1984: 181). It includes those who migrated to Britain from the Indian sub-continent with capital specifically to extend their existing business interests, along with that small proportion of Asians expelled from East Africa who have been able to reproduce their bourgeois class position in Britain. In addition, a small proportion of Asians have, by a combination of wage income and commercial transactions, accumulated sufficient wealth to establish themselves initially as members of the *petite bourgeoisie* and subsequently as employers of wage labour (Nowikowski 1984, Wilson 1983).

The view that Asian and Caribbean people in Britain collectively constitute a 'black' underclass, a collectivity homogenous in its poverty and economic disadvantage relative to 'white' people as a result of racism and systematic exclusionary practices, is therefore mistaken (Rex and Tomlinson 1979: 1-35, Sivanandan 1982: 11, 123). Nevertheless, on several dimensions, the economic position occupied by a large proportion of Asian and Caribbean people is inferior to that of the indigenous population. Of those who occupy a proletarian economic position, Caribbean and Asian men are much less likely to be employed in non-manual jobs than indigenous men are, and within manual employment, they are much more likely to be engaged in semi- and unskilled jobs (Brown 1984: 157-65). And concerning the relative surplus population, official data, for all its limitations, shows that unemployment rates for people of Asian and Caribbean origin collectively are higher than for the indigenous population (Newnham 1986: 9-12). This implies, although it does not demonstrate, that racism and related exclusionary practices are significant factors in the determination of the class position of people of Asian and Caribbean origin in Britain. Hence, the analytical task is to assess the manner in which racialisation and racism articulate with other processes in the allocation of persons to particular positions in the hierarchy of class relations.

The capitalist mode of production is, by comparison with other modes of production, inherently expansionary. As we have already seen, the quantitative accumulation of capital sustains a complex dialectic of relative expansion and contraction in the size of the capitalist and working classes, as well as the relative surplus population, within any single nation state. In a world economy dominated by the capitalist mode of production, this structures the temporary and permanent migration of people from one nation state to another to fill the increased number of manual and administrative positions. Moreover, capitalists as well as capital have been mobile across national boundaries. However, since the early 1970s and the onset of a major crisis in the accumulation process, international migration into Western Europe has been much reduced and the size of the relative surplus population within Western Europe has considerably increased as people have been expelled from the labour force. In this broad structural cycle of accumulation, there has occurred a complex process of inclusion and exclusion of people in and from the different sites of class relations as the size of these sites has expanded and contracted.

A variety of criteria is utilised to effect these processes of inclusion and exclusion. Historically, the signification of sexual difference has been central to the inclusion and exclusion of people in and from wage labour. In certain historical conjunctures, women have been actively encouraged to enter wage labour and in others they have been actively discouraged (see Bland *et al.* 1978). Moreover, this instance of signification has served to allocate women to specific positions within the hierarchy of wage labour, for example, to exclude them from positions of skill and heavy manual labour and from positions which receive relatively high wages (Oakley 1981: 150-62). In conjunction with migration, the signification of phenotypical difference has also been central to the inclusion and exclusion of people in and from wage labour, and to the allocation of people to the range of different sites in the hierarchy of wage labour as I shall now demonstrate with reference to the example of Britain.

The British economy, in common with all other Western European economies, experienced significant shortages of labour in the 1940s and 1950s in the context of a new phase of capital accumulation and the reorganisation of the labour market after the Second World War. But, unlike all other Western European economies, a vast majority of migrants who entered Britain during the 1940s and 1950s to fill these vacant positions came either from colonies and ex-colonies and were British subjects who were not at the time subject to immigration control or were citizens of the Republic of Ireland who were given privileged access to the British labour market. Consequently, unlike all other Western European nation states, there was no extensive use of a migrant labour system based on the issue of work and residence permits by the state (Castles *et al.* 1984: 20-8). With certain notable exceptions (for example, Brooks 1975, Harris 1987), the migration proceeded by informal means, but was regulated by the condition of the labour market (Peach 1968). This relationship broke down with the imposition of immigration controls on British subjects born in the Commonwealth in 1962 and 1965 (although citizens of the Irish Republic were excluded from these controls). Thereafter, migrants from the Caribbean and Indian subcontinent were mainly dependants of those who had arrived during the 1950s in order to find paid work, although in the late 1960s and again in the early 1970s, they were joined by migrants from East Africa who were, in effect, political refugees (for example, Twaddle 1975).

The vast majority of the migrants of the 1950s arrived with little or no capital and therefore had no choice but to sell their labour power for a wage, even where their intentions were to accumulate capital. Because only a small proportion were specifically recruited before their migration to particular jobs, most arrived to fill positions either found for them by kin and friends or by themselves. There were some significant exceptions to this migration process. First, a small minority of migrants, mainly from the Indian subcontinent, arrived with some capital and the intention of extending their existing capitalist interests within Britain (Nowikowski 1984). Second, another small minority of migrants arrived to fill professional positions, most notably within the National Health Service as doctors (Unit for Manpower Studies 1977: 58-61). If we ignore these exceptions, we are left to explain the reasons why so many migrants from the Indian subcontinent and the Caribbean filled semi- and unskilled positions in manual wage labour.

A key part of the explanation lies in the fact that these were positions that were vacant as a result of the movement of indigenous labour into 'new jobs' characterised by higher rates of pay and better conditions of work. In the course of the post-war restructuring of the British economy, the expansion of light engineering and consumer durable industries, and of the service sector entailed the creation of new areas of wage labour employment, while older sectors of production (such as textile production and metal manufacture) faced increasing international competition and a worsening of the conditions of work (for example, Fevre 1984: 17-54, Duffield 1985: 144-52). Consequently, certain economic sectors faced acute shortages of labour, and in conditions of relative full employment, these positions could not be filled from the population within Britain. Thus, structural circumstances defined a demand for labour in certain sectors of the economy, and it was these positions that Caribbean and Asian migrants filled.

But this does not constitute the totality of the explanation. Unlike migrant labour recruited by a contract system whereby a contract locates the migrant in a specific position in the hierarchy of wage labour and confines the migrant to that position for a specific period of time, Caribbean and Asian migrants were in theory free to sell their labour power to whomever they wished. They were therefore free to compete with indigenous labour for access to the expanding number of new, higher paid jobs with better conditions. Thus, the explanation for the fact that, during the 1950s and 1960s, most Caribbean and Asian workers were employed in semi-skilled or unskilled manual work that placed them in an inferior position within the ranks of manual wage labour requires an additional level of explanation. We find this in the fact that the process of labour recruitment has a representational dimension because (as we have already seen in this chapter) it depends on an employer's conception of the abilities and skills required for the job to be effectively carried out, and of the abilities and skills of the people who offer their labour power for sale. The employer tries to match the perceived qualities of the applicants to the perceived requirements of the job in question. The employer's evaluation of these qualities and requirements therefore functions as criteria of inclusion and exclusion in that they serve to differentiate all those who seek jobs.

Consequently, those people present in the labour market are ranked by employers. Where that hierarchy is constructed in such a way that the qualities of individuals are perceived to be representative of a wider collectivity, and if the individual is deemed to possess the criteria that designate membership of such collectivity, the question of suitability may be determined by reference to the perceived qualities of the collectivity rather than to the perceived qualities of the individual applicant. In such circumstances, the processes of inclusion and exclusion are effected by signification and group categorisation. Where such a process is effected by reference to phenotypical characteristics, the recruitment of labour is racialised. That is, the labour market is perceived to include members of different 'races', each of which is seen to possess a range of different skills and abilities which distinguish that group as a supposed 'race'.

Since the 1950s, the British labour market has been racialised in this way. Employers have signified certain physical and cultural characteristics (notably skin colour, and hence the designation 'coloured labour' or 'coloured workers') of Caribbean and Asian migrants and their British-born children and this signification has structured recruitment processes. They believed not only that the labour market consisted of a number of different 'races' but also that these 'races' had different characteristics which influenced their employability. During the 1950s and early 1960s, this process of racialisation was accompanied by the exclusion of these migrants in two ways (Wright 1968: 212). First, many employers refused to employ any 'coloured' workers, and most would only do so where there was no other source of labour power available. In other words, in a racialised labour market, British employers consistently excluded Asian and Caribbean workers while 'white' labour was available. Second, where Caribbean and Asian migrants were employed, they were nevertheless excluded from certain sorts of job, or their numbers in the workforce were often limited to accord with a predetermined quota.

What were the reasons for this exclusionary practice? Part of the explanation lies in the fact that the majority of migrants, including those who considered themselves skilled in the context of the forces and relations of production in the Caribbean and the Indian subcontinent, had few skills relevant to an industrial capitalist economy (Wright 1968: 30-40) and, on this criterion, were likely to be excluded from any form of skilled manual or non-manual employment. But racism was also a motivating factor. Some employers explained their exclusionary practices by reference to the anticipated or real opposition of their existing workforce to working with 'coloureds', opposition that they endorsed by acting in this manner. Others negatively stereotyped Asians as 'slow to learn', or West Indians as lazy, unresponsive to discipline and truculent, or 'coloured people' generally as prone to accidents or requiring more supervision than 'white' workers (Wright 1968: 89-144). In all these instances, migrants were signified by skin colour and attributed collectively with negatively evaluated characteristics. Not all employers in Wright's survey articulated such racist views and so unanimity should not be assumed. Nevertheless, the interrelationship between the racialisation of migrants, racism and exclusionary practice set limits to the parameters of the labour market open to migrants from the Caribbean and Indian subcontinent. Thus, while the accumulation process determined a demand for an addition to the size of the British working class, and thereby stimulated migration, racism and associated exclusionary practices both placed those migrants in, and largely restricted them to, semi- and unskilled positions in the manual working class.

This interrelationship between racialisation, racism and exclusionary practice has continued to constitute a structural constraint for people of Asian and Caribbean origin seeking wage labour, thereby maintaining a hierarchy of concordance and setting ideological limits to the operation of the labour market. Three major studies on the nature and extent of exclusionary practice (Daniel 1968, Smith 1977, Brown 1984) have demonstrated that acts of exclusion of Asian and Caribbean people when searching for work remain widespread, although they have become more covert since they were made illegal in 1968. A more recent study by Jenkins (1986) demonstrates that there is wide scope for racialisation and racism to structure the decisions of managers in the course of the recruitment of workers, and therefore to determine their position in the labour market. From the theoretical perspective adopted here, the study is problematic by virtue of utilising an inflated concept of racism (Jenkins 1986: 5) and by presupposing the nature of the common-sense categories employed by managers in conceptualising workers of Caribbean and Asian origin (1986: 80); this presupposition prompted them to employ ethnic/national categories and therefore probably explains why his respondents signified cultural rather than phenotypical characteristics (1986: 94).

Nevertheless, Jenkins shows that, when making decisions about the recruitment of labour, a majority of managers do so with a set of racist stereotypes and with a set of more general negative beliefs about Caribbean and Asian workers which are similar to the common themes of contemporary racism in Britain (1986: 83-4, 107-9). Thus, they tend to regard 'immigration' as generally a 'bad thing', to define workers of Caribbean and Asian origin as 'not-British', and to believe that there are 'too many of them' in Britain. In addition, it was common for managers to believe that the employment of Asian and Caribbean workers created a number of problems for them or for their organisation (1986: 95-105). Finally, Jenkins demonstrates that several of the criteria of acceptability sought by managers when recruiting workers lead to the systematic exclusion of applicants of Caribbean and Asian origin (1986: 79). Moreover, these criteria, beliefs and assumptions are held in a context where the predominant methods of identifying job applicants are to conduct a search within the organisation or by 'word of mouth', procedures which provide considerable scope for racism to sustain exclusionary practices (1986: 134-5).

I am arguing that it is mistaken both to characterise the population of Caribbean and Asian origin in Britain in the 1980s as occupying a unitary class position, and to explain the economic positions of this population as the sole consequence of racism and exclusionary practice. This can be further demonstrated by considering the reasons for the increasing proportion of Asian people who occupy a *petit-bourgeois* class position in Britain. In common with many economically induced migrations, Asian migration to Britain has been motivated in part by a desire not only for economic advancement but also for entry into the *petite bourgeoisie*. For example, a large proportion of the Patidars who originate from Gujarat in India arrived in Britain, from India and from East Africa, with a merchant ideology. Thus, although the vast majority of these migrants entered British economic relations as sellers of labour power, they retained the intention of self-employment in some form of trading activity. Not all, and perhaps only a minority, have managed to effect this transition, but for those who have, it is a transition that is shaped in part by the intentions and objectives that originally motivated the migration (Tambs-Lyche 1980: 57, 60, 125). The implications of this motivation for movement into the *petite bourgoisie* on the part of Asian migrants and their children have been reinforced for some by the experience of racism and exclusionary practice, the belief being that self-employment will serve at least to insulate them from such experiences within the labour market (Forester 1978: 420-3, Anwar 1979: 125, Nowikowski 1984: 158, 164). In this instance, individual motivations and cultural traditions have been overdetermined by racism and exclusionary practices in placing them in economic relations.

The reproduction of the capitalist mode of production depends upon the continuous and successful allocation of people to the various sites within economic relations, the number and nature of which are determined by the accumulation process. This is the context in which a number of inclusionary and exclusionary practices occur, each dependent upon a process of signification. These processes of signification can be expressive of racism, sexism and nationalism, either singly or in some combination. For those with only their labour power to sell, they have few choices other than to enter the labour market, within which they may attempt to seek out the most favourable conditions. The demand for labour power (which has a quantitative and qualitative dimension) is the central structural determinant of the allocative process, determining the scope for signification and exclusion. But wherever supply exceeds demand within any sector of the labour market, for whatever reason, exclusion in some form will necessarily occur.

CONCLUSION

In this chapter, and in the light of the arguments of the preceding chapters, I have suggested that a primary analytical task is the historical investigation of the interpolation of racialisation and racism in political and economic relations in concrete social formations. In the course of such investigations, one should presuppose that racism is a necessarily contradictory phenomenon rather than that it is functional to the mode of production. I believe that such an analysis highlights both the specificity and the generality of the historical development of the capitalist mode of production, and I have illustrated this argument by means of three different instances.

First, the reproduction and constitution of non- and pre-capitalist relations of production is a common dimension of the development of the capitalist mode of production (Wolpe 1980, Meillassoux 1981). In certain historical instances, these processes have been effected partially by the interpolation of racialisation and racism. For example, in the case of late nineteenth and early twentieth century Kenya, we have seen how these processes led to the construction of the idea of a hierarchy of human 'races' in order actively to synchronise (and then to justify) the distribution of Africans (represented as a biologically inferior Other) to particular sites of production. Hence, the ideology of racism was not so much a *post hoc* legitimation of the placement of people in, and the confinement of people to, particular positions in the relations of production. Rather, it actively structured economic relations in a specific manner in order to bring about and reproduce a spatially and economically integrated system of production which involved an articulation of free and unfree labour. Consequently, we cannot explain the effectivity of racism in colonial Kenya without taking account of the economic constraints of the conjuncture whereby the colonial ruling class required a source of labour power in a context where the African population retained access to the means of production. The mechanisms used by the colonial ruling class to force a section of the African population to make labour power available were not purely economic, but included the use of political power in the form of the colonial state and the ideology of racism.

Many other instances could have been chosen to illustrate the articulation of capitalism, colonialism and unfree labour effected by racialisation and racism (Miles 1987a). In all of these instances, the articulation has involved contradictions. In the case of Kenya, for example, the expression of racism in the colony in conjunction with the use of the power of the colonial state to force Africans to provide labour power was contradicted by the concerns of the British state in London to present its colonial policy to an international audience as based on the principles of liberalism and humanitarianism. In the case of Australia, racialised indentured labour suited the needs of landowners

organising tropical agricultural production in Queensland, but roused the
opposition of wage labourers of European origin, concerned to protect their
labour market position, and of other landowners anxious to constitute and
reproduce an independent nation state who believed that the presence of
'coloured races' obstructed the development of national identity and the
democratic process.

Second, the historical complimentarity between the specifically economic
form of capitalist relations of production (the capital/wage labour relationship) and the political form of the nation state has generated an ideology
which attempts to make a sense of imagined community a basis for political
stability. Nationalism has therefore become a general feature of the spread of
the capitalist mode of production, being both product and determinant of that
expansion. And, as we have seen in the case of Europe, and specifically
Britain, nationalism has articulated with racism in historically specific
instances. The interpolation of racialisation and racism is therefore one
ideological form by which to include and exclude human beings within the
political collectivity of the nation state. The analysis of that specific articulation, which seeks to explain its nature and origin in the characteristics of the
specific historical instance, is also an analysis of the general political process
of nation-state formation and reproduction and its interrelation with the
process of capitalist development.

Again, the contradictory consequences of the expression of racism in the
context of the reproduction of the nation state should be highlighted. For
example, throughout north west Europe since 1945, the state has permitted or
actively facilitated migration in order to resolve a labour shortage in certain
sectors of the economy which threatened to hinder the reproduction of the
capitalist mode of production. The resulting migration into the nation states
of north west Europe and continuing demand for their labour power have
resulted in the permanent settlement of a proportion of the migrants, whose
presence has nevertheless been problematised and has therefore become the
object of political debate. Some contributors to that debate have racialised the
migrant presence and have demanded that the state implement certain
exclusionary practices. In turn, the expression of racism and the im-
plementation of exclusionary practices have stimulated defensive activities by
groups of migrant settlers. The consequence has been a spiral of action and
reaction, and therefore of political conflict, which the state has to attempt to
mediate and suppress. Thus, inclusionary practices initially effected by the
state in the interests of employers facing labour shortages have been
contradicted by the political agitation of those who have racialised the migrant
presence and who have defined it as a disintegrative influence.

Third, I have considered the processes by which individuals are allocated
to the hierarchy of positions of production and reproduction within capitalist

relations of production. Wherever the number of available persons is in excess of the available positions, some form of exclusionary practice grounded in a process of signification is necessary. Thus, within the capitalist mode of production, the ideology of sexism has justified the exclusion of large numbers of women from the labour market and their confinement to the various tasks involved in the reproduction of the labour force by means of unpaid domestic labour. In a similar manner, the racialisation of a population establishes a hierarchy of suitability and the ideological basis for exclusionary practices. Thus, in the instance of Britain, the post-1945 labour market was racialised by the state and employers after migration from the Caribbean and the Indian subcontinent, and racism (in conjunction with a number of other factors) has played a key role in excluding substantial minorities of workers of Asian and Caribbean origin from skilled manual and non-manual occupations and from the labour market itself. But, again, the effectivity of racism has to be evaluated in relation to the fact that a differentiated labour market and a relative surplus population are structural features of capitalist societies: racism and exclusionary practices only have their determinate effects because of these structural features.

This too has contradictory dimensions. Within a capitalist society, unemployment and semi- and unskilled manual occupations are structurally essential to its reproduction, but the consequence of racism and related exclusionary practices, which have the effect of placing and confining certain groups of people to such positions, can be to encourage the development of political resistance which can lead, in turn, to conflicts of various sorts. This requires the intervention of the state, perhaps leading to increased state expenditure, to mediate the resulting disorder. However, subsequent attempts by the state to minimise or eliminate racism and exclusionary practices in order to prevent further resistance on the part of those excluded by racism can only lead to the adoption of alternative processes of signification and exclusion.

Conclusion

A central objective of this book has been to justify the retention of racism as a key concept within the social sciences. Having established theoretically a concept of racism as an ideology which is not restricted by being grounded in a single empirical instance, and having linked that concept with that of racialisation, I believe that it is possible to extend the scope of the analysis of racism beyond the current, rather narrow, focus on contemporary conjunctures in single social formations and beyond the conception of racism as a singular product of the interrelationship between capitalism and colonialism. It therefore becomes possible to undertake the task of analysing the many different racisms that other writers have referred to but have done little so far to identify and explain. But there is only limited value in analysing them in themselves.

A simple description of the different forms that racism has taken historically has use primarily as a catalogue for the history of certain ideas. Such a catalogue does, however, prepare the ground for the more important and difficult analytical task of explaining the historically specific articulations of racialisation and racism within political and economic relations. Thus, the real challenge is to place the concepts of racialisation and racism at the centre of a historical, as well as a contemporary, sociology which is concerned with the origin and development of, as well as the current structure and process of, the capitalist mode of production (a development which involves a continuing articulation with non-capitalist modes of production).

In conducting that analysis, and in the light of the arguments of this book, there should be a sensitivity to three aspects of the nature of the expression of racism. First, as an ideology, it is necessary to delineate the complexity of its reproduction. This means, in particular, avoiding any assumption of simple, historical duplication. Ideologies are never only received but are also constructed and reconstructed by people responding to their material and cultural circumstances in order to comprehend, represent and act in relation to those circumstances. Ideological reproduction is therefore a consequence of a transaction between historical legacy and individual and collective attempts to make sense of the world.

There are important consequences. The specific content of racism should be expected to change temporally and contextually. A discourse 'inherited' from the past is likely to be reconstituted if it is to be used to make sense of the world in a new context, while new circumstances can be expected to stimulate the formation of new representations. Moreover, the expression of racism should be distinguished analytically from the reception of racism. Studies of the discourse of racism articulated by journalists, editors, writers, scientists, priests and politicians are common and are relatively easily conducted where these discourses take a written form, as is demonstrated by the relatively numerous studies of the development of scientific racism and of the manner in which racism is articulated in newspapers. But it is too often assumed that the *expression* of racism is synonymous with the communication of racism, in which the audience necessarily comprehends and accepts the ideology that has been identified as present.

It does not automatically follow that the expression of racism in a newspaper will result in all its readers articulating a racist message. That this is a mistaken assumption is demonstrated by the existence of researchers who are able to identify and question this ideology. Moreover, if it were true, there would be little or no scope for anti-racist intervention. Consequently, considerably more attention should be devoted to identifying and explaining the active construction and reproduction of racism amongst people in different class locations, and the reception and rejection of racism by the audiences of the mass media and politicians, etc.

The second aspect is that the effects of its expression always articulate with the extant economic and political relations as well as other ideologies. Thus, although there may be formal (or political) reasons to attempt to assess the independent impact of the expression of racism, it should always be remembered that those who articulate it and those who are its object are located in a wider, complex web of social relations. Consequently, the expression of racism may be the result of an attempt to secure other interests and outcomes and its effects may be contextualised by other facets of people's economic and political circumstances. Moreover, where those who are its object do share in other respects a structural position with others who are not similarly affected, or differ in other respects from those who are similarly affected, it is necessary to demonstrate that the outcome attributed to the effects of racism has not been partially or wholly determined by some aspect of the shared structural position or by the other differences between them. It should be emphasised once more that to argue this is not to deny but rather to contextualise the effectivity of racism.

There is an important implication. Racism and related exclusionary practices have their own specificity and give rise to particular, exclusive experiences. But the material consequence or outcome, the fact of exclusion, may be shared with others. For example, I have shown that racism has played an important role in excluding a significant minority of people of Caribbean and Asian origin from skilled manual and non-manual work, and indeed from the labour market in Britain. But these are not the only people excluded from skilled manual and non-manual work or from the labour market. In a context of fluctuating and relative scarcity, where the total number of jobs within a nation state is less than the total population seeking paid work and where the number of skilled manual and non-manual positions is even less, exclusionary practices are structurally required, but may be effected by means of, for example, some combination of sexism, racism, and nationalism as well as the formal possession of acquired skills. Similarly, in capitalist societies which are unable to provide sufficient and adequate housing for their populations, some mechanism of inclusion/exclusion is necessary to allocate people to housing of poor quality and racism is one amongst a number of such mechanisms. By seeking to contextualise the impact of racism within class relations, one can begin to contextualise the specificity of the experience of racism, not in order to deny it, but rather in order simultaneously to highlight and generalise it by means of demonstrating the linkages with other means of exclusion.

Third, formal theoretical generalisations about the nature and conse-quences of the expression of racism should be able to account for their 'multidimensionality' and their 'historical specificity'. I have emphasised that the articulation of racism always has a number of economic, political, and representational consequences, some of which can be contradictory. More-over, the nature of those consequences changes historically, partly in accord-ance with different class interests and strategies, different strategies of resistance, and different material and cultural contexts. Definitions of racism which, attribute the ideology with an ontologically and exclusively funct-ional, economic and colonial character systematically obscure its multi-dimensionality and specificity. Simplistic analysis, not surprisingly, gives rise to simple solutions, and the continuing articulation of racism, when seen against the background of its long historical genesis, is sufficient testimony to the limitations of such analyses.

Further reading

While detailed references are listed in the Bibliography, a short, general guide to the relevant literature is useful to structure further reading.

The most influential sociological texts dealing with the concept of racism are:

Zubaida S. (ed.) (1970) *Race and Racialism*, London: Tavistock.

Blauner R. (1972) *Racial Oppression in America*, New York: Harper & Row.

Wellman D. (1977) *Portraits of White Racism*, Cambridge: Cambridge University Press.

Van den Berghe P. L. (1978) *Race and Racism: A Comparative Perspective*, New York: Wiley.

Rex J. (1970) *Race Relations in Sociological Theory*, London: Weidenfeld & Nicolson.

Benedict R. (1983) *Race and Racism*, London: Routledge and Kegan Paul.

For historical and critical analyses of the idea of 'race', see:

Barzun J. (1938) *Race: A Study in Modern Superstition*, London: Methuen.

Montagu M. (ed.) (1964) *The Concept of Race*, New York: Free Press.

Montagu M. (ed.) (1972) *Statement on Race*, London: Oxford University Press.

Gould S. J. (1984) *The Mismeasure of Man*, Harmondsworth: Penguin.

Banton M. (1987) *Racial Theories*, Cambridge: Cambridge University Press.

The most important Marxist writings which analyse the concept of racism are:

Cox O. C. (1970) *Caste, Class and Race*, New York: Monthly Review Press.

Hall S. (1980) 'Race, Articulation and Societies Structured in Dominance', in UNESCO, *Sociological Theories: Race and Colonialism*, Paris: UNESCO.

Barker M. (1981) *The New Racism*, London: Junction Books.

Miles R. (1982) *Racism and Migrant Labour: A Critical Text*, London: Routledge & Kegan Paul.

Solomos J. (1986) 'Varieties of Marxist Conceptions of "Race", Class and the State', in Rex J. and Mason D. (eds) *Theories of Race and Ethnic Relations*, Cambridge: Cambridge University Press.

On the historical genesis of racism, see:

Hirschfeld M. (1938) *Racism*, London: Gollancz.

Curtin P. D. (1965) *The Image of Africa: British Ideas and Action, 1780-1850*, London: Macmillan.

Jordan W. J. (1968) *White Over Black: American Attitudes Toward the Negro, 1550-1812*, Chapel Hill: University of North Carolina Press.

Curtis L. P. (1968) *Anglo-Saxons and Celts*, Connecticut: University of Bridgeport Press.

Barker A. J. (1978) *The African Link: British Attitudes to the Negro in the Era of the Atlantic Slave Trade, 1550-1807*, London: Frank Cass.

Mosse G. L. (1978) *Toward the Final Solution: A History of European Racism*, London: Dent & Sons.

Fryer P. (1984) *Staying Power: The History of Black People in Britain*, London: Pluto Press.

Said E. (1985) *Orientalism*, Harmondsworth: Penguin.

For an overview of 'race relations' studies, see:

Banton M. (1983) *Racial and Ethnic Competition*, Cambridge: Cambridge University Press.

Rex J. and Mason D. (eds) (1986) *Theories of Race and Ethnic Relations*, Cambridge: Cambridge University Press.

Alternative Marxist analyses of migration which highlight the significance of racism are:

Phizacklea A. (ed.) (1983) *One-Way Ticket: Migration and Female Labour*, London: Routledge & Kegan Paul.

Miles R. and Phizacklea A. (1984) *White Man's Country: Racism in British Politics*, London: Pluto Press.

Castles S., Booth H., and Wallace T. (1984) *Here for Good: Western Europe's New Ethnic Minorities*, London: Pluto Press.

Miles R. (1987) *Capitalism and Unfree Labour: Anomaly or Necessity?*, London: Tavistock.

Cohen R. (1987) *The New Helots*, Farnborough: Avebury.

The most important radical, 'black' analyses of racism include:

Sivanandan A. (1982) *A Different Hunger: Writings on Black Resistance*, London: Pluto Press.

Centre for Contemporary Cultural Studies (CCCS) (1982) *The Empire Strikes Back: Race and Racism in 70s Britain*, London: Hutchinson.

Robinson C. J. (1983) *Black Marxism*, London: Zed Press.

Omi M. and Winant H. (1986) *Racial Formation in the United States: From the 1960s to the 1980s*, London: Routledge & Kegan Paul.

For discussion of the interrelation between racism and nationalism, see:

Poliakov L. (1974) *The Aryan Myth: A History of Racist and Nationalist Ideas in Europe*, London: Heinemann.

Nairn T. (1981) *The Break-Up of Britain*, London: Verso.

Anderson B. (1983) *Imagined Communities: Reflections on the Origin and Spread of Nationalism*, London: Verso.

Wright P. (1985) *On Living in An Old Country*, London: Verso.

Miles R. (1987) 'Recent Marxist Theories of Nationalism and the Issue of Racism', *British Journal of Sociology*, 38,1: 24-43.

For discussion of the interrelation between racism and sexism, see:

Carby H.V. (1982) 'White Women Listen! Black Feminism and the Boundaries of Sisterhood', in CCCS, *The Empire Strikes Back*, London: Hutchinson.

Brittan A. and Maynard M. (1984) *Sexism, Racism and Oppression*, Oxford: Basil Blackwell.

Anthias F. and Yuval-Davis N. (1983) 'Contextualising Feminism: Gender, Ethnic and Class Divisions', *Feminist Review*, 15: 62-75.

de Lepervanche M. (1988) 'Racism and Sexism in Australian National Life', in de Lepervanche M. and Bottomley G. (eds) *The Cultural Construction of Race*, Sydney: Sydney Association for Studies in Society and Culture.

On racism and the New Right, see:

Palmer F. (ed.) (1986) *Anti-Racism – An Assault on Education and Value*, London: Sherwood Press.

Levitas R. (ed.) (1986) *The Ideology of the New Right*, London: Polity Press.

Bibliography

Allen, S. (1973) 'The Institutionalisation of Racism', *Race* 15, 1: 99-106.

ALTARF (All London Teachers Against Racism and Fascism) (1984) *Challenging Racism*, London: ALTARF.

Amos, V. and Parmar, P. (1984) 'Challenging Imperial Feminism', *Feminist Review*, 17: 3-19.

Anderson, B. (1983) *Imagined Communities: Reflections on the Origin and Spread of Nationalism*, London: Verso.

Anon. (1983) 'Ethnic Origin and Economic Status', *Employment Gazette*, 91: 424-30.

—— (1987) 'Ethnic Origin and Economic Status', *Employment Gazette*, 95: 18-29.

Anstey, R. (1975) *The Atlantic Slave Trade and British Abolition 1760-1810*, London: Macmillan.

Anthias, F. (1983) 'Sexual Divisions and Ethnic Adaptation: The Case of Greek-Cypriot Women', in A. Phizacklea (ed.) *One-Way Ticket*, London: Routledge & Kegan Paul.

—— and Yuval-Davies, N. (1983) 'Contextualising Feminism: Gender, Ethnic and Class Divisions', *Feminist Review*, 15: 62-75.

Anwar, M. (1979) *The Myth of Return: Pakistanis in Britain*, London: Heinemann.

Arens, W. (1979) *The Man-Eating Myth: Anthropology and Anthropophagy*, New York: Oxford University Press.

Baldry, H.C. (1965) *The Unity of Mankind in Greek Thought*, Cambridge: Cambridge University Press.

Banton, M. (1970) 'The Concept of Racism', in S. Zubaida (ed.) *Race and Racialism*, London: Tavistock.

—— (1977) *The Idea of Race*, London: Tavistock.

—— (1980) 'The Idiom of Race: A Critique of Presentism', *Research in Race and Ethnic Relations*, 2: 21-42.

—— (1987) *Racial Theories*, Cambridge: Cambridge University Press.

Barber, A. (1985) 'Ethnic Origin and Economic Status', *Employment Gazette*, 93: 467-77.

Barker, A.J. (1978) *The African Link: British Attitudes to the Negro in the Era of the Atlantic Slave Trade, 1550-1807*, London: Frank Cass.

Barker, M. (1981) *The New Racism*, London: Junction Books.

Barrett, M. (1980) *Women's Oppression Today: Problems in Marxist Feminist Analysis*, London: Verso.

—— and McIntosh, M. (1985) 'Ethnocentrism and Socialist-Feminist Theory', *Feminist Review*, 20: 23-47.

Barzun, J. (1938) *Race: A Study in Modern Superstition*, London: Methuen.

Bastide, R. (1968) 'Color, Racism, and Christianity', in J.H. Franklin (ed.) *Color and Race*, Boston: Houghton Mifflin Company.

Baudet, H. (1976) *Paradise on Earth: Some Thoughts on European Images of Non-European Man*, Westport: Greenwood Press.

Bearce, G.D. (1982) *British Attitudes Towards India, 1784-1858*, Westport: Greenwood Press.

Beddoe, J. (1885) *The Races of Britain: A Contribution to the Anthropology of Western Europe*, Bristol: J.W. Arrowsmith.

Benedict, R. (1983) *Race and Racism*, London: Routledge & Kegan Paul.

Bennett, G. (1965) 'Settlers and Politics in Kenya', in V. Harlow and E.M. Chiver (eds) *History of East Africa*, vol. II, Oxford: Clarendon Press.

Bhavnani, K.K. and Coulson, M. (1986) 'Transforming Socialist-Feminism: the Challenge of Racism', *Feminist Review*, 23: 81-92.

Biddiss, M. (1975) 'Myths of the Blood: European Racist Ideology 1850-1945', *Patterns of Prejudice*, 9, 5: 11-19.

—— (1979a) 'Towards a History of European Racism', *Ethnic and Racial Studies*, 2, 4: 508-13.

—— (1979b) *Images of Race*, Leicester: Leicester University Press.

Billig, M. (1976) *Social Psychology and Intergroup Relations*, London: Academic Press.

—— (1978) *Fascists: A Social Psychological View of the National Front*, London: Harcourt Brace Jovanovich.

—— (1982) *Ideology and Social Psychology*, Oxford: Basil Blackwell.

Blainey, G. (1984) *All for Australia*, Sydney: Methuen Haynes.

Blair, T.L. (1977) *Retreat from the Ghetto: The End of a Dream?*, New York: Hill and Wang.

Bland, L., Brunsdon, C., Hobson, D., and Winship, J. (1978) 'Women "Inside and Outside" the Relations of Production', in Women's Studies Group *Women Take Issue: Aspects of Women's Subordination*, London: Hutchinson.

Blauner, R. (1972) *Racial Oppression in America*, New York: Harper & Row.

Boas, F. (1940) *Race, Culture and Language*, New York: Free Press.

Bodmer, W.F. (1972) 'Race and IQ: the genetic background', in K. Richardson, D. Spears and M. Richards (eds) *Race, Culture and Intelligence*, Harmondsworth: Penguin.

Bolt, C. (1969) *The Anti-Slavery Movement and Reconstruction: A Study in Anglo-American Co-operation 1833-77*, London: Oxford University Press.

—— (1971) *Victorian Attitudes to Race*, London: Routledge & Kegan Paul.

Boyd, W.C. (1950) *Genetics and the Races of Man: An Introduction to Modern Physical Anthropology*, Oxford: Basil Blackwell.

Braudel, F. (1984) *Civilisation and Capitalism: 15th-18th Century: Volume III, The Perspective of the World*, London: Collins.

Brett, E.A. (1973) *Colonialism and Underdevelopment in East Africa: The Politics of Economic Change, 1919-1939*, London: Heinemann.

Brink, A. (1983) *A Chain of Voices*, London: Fontana.

Brooks, D. (1975) *Race and Labour in London Transport*, London: Oxford University Press.

Brown, C. (1984) *Black and White Britain: The Third PSI Study*, London: Heinemann.

Cairns, H.A.C. (1965) *Prelude to Imperialism: British Reactions to Central African Society*, London: Routledge & Kegan Paul.

Carmichael, S. and Hamilton, C.V. (1968) *Black Power: The Politics of Liberation in America*, London: Jonathan Cape.

Carter, B, Harris, C., and Joshi, S. (1987) 'The 1951-55 Conservative Government and the Racialisation of Black Immigration', *Immigrants and Minorities*, 6: 335-47.

Cashmore, E. (1986) *The Logic of Racism*, London: Allen & Unwin.

Castles, S., Booth, H., and Wallace, T. (1984) *Here for Good: Western Europe's New Ethnic Minorities*, London: Pluto Press.

Castles, S. and Kosack, G. (1972) 'The Function of Labour Immigration in Western European Capitalism', *New Left Review*, 73: 3-21.

Centre for Contemporary Cultural Studies (CCCS) (1982) *The Empire Strikes Back: Race and Racism in 70s Britain*, London: Hutchinson.

Chachage, C.S.L. (1988) 'British Rule and African Civilisation in Tanganyika', *Journal of Historical Sociology*, forthcoming.

Clark, L.L. (1984) *Social Darwinism in France*, Birmingham: University of Alabama Press.

—— (1988) 'Le Darwinisme Social en France', *La Recherche*, 19: 192-200.

Clayton, A. and Savage, D.C. (1974) *Government and Labour in Kenya, 1895-1963*, London: Frank Cass.

Coard, B. (1971) *How the West Indian Child is Made Educationally Subnormal in the British School System*, London: New Beacon Books.

Cole, R.G. (1972) 'Sixteenth Century Travel Books as a Source of European Attitudes Toward Non-White and Non-Western Culture', *Proceedings of the American Philosophical Society*, 116: 59-67.

Comas, J. (1961) '"Scientific" Racism Again?', *Current Anthropology*, 2: 303-40.

Combe, G. (1830) *System of Phrenology*, Edinburgh: John Anderson.

—— (1836) *The Constitution of Man Considered in Relation to External Objects*, Edinburgh: Maclachlan and Stewart.

Connell, R.W. and Irving, T.H. (1980) *Class Structure in Australian History*, Melbourne: Longman Cheshire.

Cope, B. and Kalantzis, M. (1985) 'The Reality of a Term', *Australian Society*, July: 25-7.

Corrigan, P. and Sayer, D. (1986) *The Great Arch: English State Formation as Cultural Revolution*, Oxford: Basil Blackwell.

Cox, O.C. (1970) *Caste, Class and Race*, New York: Monthly Review Press.

Crawford, P.C. (1923) *Chinese Coolie Emigration to Countries Within the British Empire*, London: P.S. King & Son.

Curtin, P.D. (1961) '"White Man's Grave:" Image and Reality, 1780-1850', *Journal of British Studies*, 1: 94-110.

—— (1965) *The Image of Africa: British Ideas and Action, 1780-1850*, London: Macmillan.

Curtis, L.P. (1968) *Anglo-Saxons and Celts*, Connecticut: University of Bridgeport Press.

—— (1971) *Apes and Angels: the Irishman in Victorian Caricature*, Washington: Smithsonian Institution Press.

Dallas, K.M. (1955) 'The Origins of "White Australia"', *Australian Quarterly*, 27: 43-52.

Daniel, N. (1960) *Islam and the West: The Making of an Image*, Edinburgh: Edinburgh University Press.

—— (1966) *Islam, Europe and Empire*, Edinburgh: Edinburgh University Press.

—— (1975) *The Arabs and Medieval Europe*, London: Longman.

Daniel, W.W. (1968) *Racial Discrimination in England*, Harmondsworth: Penguin.

Davidowicz, L. (1977) *The War Against the Jews, 1933-45*, Harmondsworth: Penguin.

Davis, A. (1982) *Women, Race and Class*, London: The Women's Press.

Davis, D.B. (1984) *Slavery and Human Progress*, New York: Oxford University Press.

Davison, G. (1985) 'Unemployment, Race and Public Opinion: Reflections on the Asian Immigration Controversy of 1888', in A. Markus and M.C.

Ricklefs (eds) *Surrender Australia? Essays in the Study and Uses of History*, Sydney: Allen & Unwin.

DeLey, M. (1983) 'French Immigration Policy Since May 1981', *International Migration Review*, 17, 2: 196-211.

Denoon, D. (1983) *Settler Capitalism: the Dynamics of Dependent Development in the Southern Hemisphere*, Oxford: Clarendon Press.

Dickason, O.P. (1984) *The Myth of the Savage and the Beginnings of French Colonialism in the Americas*, Edmonton: University of Alberta Press.

Dijk, T.A. van (1984) *Prejudice in Discourse: An Analysis of Ethnic Prejudices in Cognition and Conversation*, Amsterdam: John Benjamins.

Duffield, M. (1985) 'Rationalisation and the Politics of Segregation: Indian Workers in Britain's Foundry Industry, 1945-62', in K. Lunn (ed.) *Race and Labour in Twentieth-Century Britain*, London: Frank Cass.

Dudley, E. and Novak, M.E. (eds) (1972) *The Wild Man Within: An Image in Western Thought from the Renaissance to Romanticism*, Pittsburgh: University of Pittsburgh Press.

Dummett, A. (1973) *A Portrait of English Racism*, Harmondsworth: Penguin.

Essien-Udom, E.U. (1962) *Black Nationalism: A Search for an Identity in America*, Chicago: University of Chicago Press.

European Economic Community (1986) *Report of the Committee of Inquiry into the Rise of Fascism and Racism in Europe*, Brussels: European Economic Community.

Evans, R. (1975) 'Race Relations in a Colonial Setting', in R. Evans, K. Saunders, and K. Cronin *Exclusion, Exploitation and Extermination: Race Relations in Colonial Queensland*, Sydney: Australia and New Zealand Book Company.

——, Saunders, K., and Cronin, K. (1975) *Exclusion, Exploitation and Extermination: Race Relations in Colonial Queensland*, Sydney: Australia and New Zealand Book Company.

Fanon, F. (1967) *The Wretched of the Earth*, Harmondsworth: Penguin.

—— (1970) *Toward the African Revolution*, Harmondsworth: Penguin.

Febvre, L. and Martin, H-J. (1976) *The Coming of the Book: The Impact of Printing, 1450-1800*, London: New Left Books.

Fevre, R. (1984) *Cheap Labour and Racial Discrimination*, Aldershot: Gower.

Field, S. (1981) *Ethnic Minorities in Britain: A Study of Trends in their Position since 1961*, London: HMSO.

Fielding, N. (1981) *The National Front*, London: Routledge & Kegan Paul.

Finley, M.I. (1980) *Ancient Slavery and Modern Ideology*, London: Chatto & Windus.

Fleming, G. (1986) *Hitler and the Final Solution*, Oxford: Oxford University Press.

Flew, A. (1986) 'Clarifying the Concepts', in F. Palmer (ed.) *Anti-Racism – An Assault on Education and Value*, London: Sherwood Press.

Forester, T. (1978) 'Asians in Business', *New Society*, 23 February: 420-3.

Fox-Genovese, E. and Genovese, E.D. (1983) *Fruits of Merchant Capital*, New York: Oxford University Press.

Fredrickson, G.M. (1972) *The Black Image in the White Mind: The Debate on Afro-American Character and Destiny, 1817-1914*, New York: Harper & Row.

Friedman, J.B. (1981) *The Monstrous Races in Medieval Art and Thought*, Cambridge, Mass.: Harvard University Press.

Fryer, P. (1984) *Staying Power: The History of Black People in Britain*, London: Pluto Press.

George, H. (1984) *American Race Relations Theory: A Review of Four Models*, Lanham: University Press of America.

George, K. (1958) 'The Civilised West Looks at Primitive Africa: 1400-1800', *Isis*, 49: 62-72.

Gergen, K.J. (1968) 'The Significance of Skin Color in Human Relations', in J.H. Franklin (ed.) *Color and Race*, Boston: Houghton Mifflin Company.

Gilroy, P. (1987) *There Ain't No Black in the Union Jack*, London: Hutchinson.

Gobineau, A. de (1970) 'Essay on the Inequality of the Human Races', in M. Biddiss (ed.) *Gobineau: Selected Political Writings*, London: Cape.

Gordon, P. (1987) 'Visas and the British Press', *Race and Class*, 28, 3: 76-80.

—— and Klug, F. (1986) *New Right New Racism*, London: Searchlight Publications.

—— and Reilly, D. (1986) 'Guestworkers of the Sea: Racism in British Shipping', *Race and Class*, 28, 2: 73-82.

Gossett, T.F. (1965) *Race: The History of an Idea in America*, New York: Schocken Books.

Gould, S.J. (1984) *The Mismeasure of Man*, Harmondsworth: Penguin.

Gramsci, A. (1971) *Selections from the Prison Notebooks*, London: Lawrence & Wishart.

Graves, A. (1986) *Race and Immigration: The 'White-Backlash' in Britain and Australia*, London: Australian Studies Centre.

Gregory, J.W. (1925) *The Menace of Colour: A Study of the Difficulties Due to the Association of White and Coloured Races, With an Account of Measures Proposed for their Solution, and Special Reference to White Colonisation in the Tropics*, London: Seeley Service & Co. Ltd.

Grillo, R.D. (1985) *Ideologies and Institutions in Urban France: The Representation of Immigrants*, Cambridge: Cambridge University Press.

Guillaumin, C. (1980) 'The Idea of Race and its Elevation to Autonomous Scientific and Legal Status', in UNESCO *Sociological Theories: Race and Colonialism*, Paris: UNESCO.

Günther, H.F.K. (1970) *The Racial Elements of European History*, New York: Kennikat Press.

Gurnah, A. (1984) 'The Politics of Racism Awareness Training', *Critical Social Policy*, 11: 6-20.

Hakluyt, R. (1972) *Voyages and Discoveries*, Harmondsworth: Penguin.

Hall, S. (1978) 'Racism and Reaction', in Commission for Racial Equality *Five Views of Multi-Racial Britain*, London: Commission for Racial Equality.

—— (1980) 'Race, Articulation and Societies Structured in Dominance', in UNESCO *Sociological Theories: Race and Colonialism*, Paris: UNESCO.

Hall, S., Critcher, C., Jefferson, T., Clarke, J., and Roberts, B. (1978) *Policing the Crisis: Mugging, the State and Law and Order*, London: Macmillan.

Haller, J.S. (1971) *Outcasts from Evolution: Scientific Attitudes of Racial Inferiority, 1859-1900*, Urbana: University of Illinois Press.

Halsey, A.H., Heath, A.F., and Ridge, J.M. (1980) *Origins and Destinations: Family, Class and Education in Modern Britain*, Oxford: Clarendon Press.

Hammar, T. (ed.) (1985) *European Immigration Policy: A Comparative Study*, Cambridge: Cambridge University Press.

Harbsmeier, M. (1985) 'Early Travels to Europe: Some Remarks on the Magic of Writing', in F. Baker (ed.) *Europe and its Others*, vol. 1, Colchester: Essex University Press.

Harris, C. (1987) 'British Capitalism, Migration and Relative Surplus-Population', *Migration*, 1, 1: 47-90.

Hartmann, P. and Husband, C. (1974) *Racism and the Mass Media*, London: Davis-Poynter.

Henriques, J. (1984) 'Social Psychology and the Politics of Racism', in J. Henriques, W. Hollway, C. Urwin, C. Venn, and V. Walkerdine *Changing the Subject: Psychology, Social Regulation and Subjectivity*, London: Methuen.

Hertz, F. (1928) *Race and Civilisation*, London: Kegan Paul, Trench, Trubner & Co.

Hibbert, C. (1984) *Africa Explored: Europeans in the Dark Continent*, Harmondsworth: Penguin.

Hilton, R. *et al.* (1978) *The Transition from Feudalism to Capitalism*, London: Verso.

Hirschfeld, M. (1938) *Racism*, London: Gollancz.

Hobsbawm, E. (1977) 'Some Reflections on "The Break-up of Britain"', *New Left Review*, 105: 3-23.

—— (1983) 'Introduction: Inventing Traditions', in E. Hobsbawm and T. Ranger (eds) *The Invention of Tradition*, Cambridge: Cambridge University Press.

Hoel, B. (1982) 'Contemporary Clothing "Sweatshops": Asian Female Labour and Collective Organisation', in J. West (ed.) *Work, Women and the Labour Market*, London: Routledge & Kegan Paul.

Holton, R.J. (1985) *The Transition from Feudalism to Capitalism*, London: Macmillan.

Honeyford, R. (1986) 'Anti-Racist Rhetoric', in F. Palmer (ed.) *Anti-Racism – An Assault on Education and Value*, London: Sherwood Press.

Hooton, E.A. (1947) *Up From the Ape*, New York: Macmillan.

Horsman, R. (1976) 'Origins of Racial Anglo-Saxonism in Great Britain Before 1850', *Journal of the History of Ideas*, 37, 3: 387-410.

—— (1981) *Race and Manifest Destiny: The Origins of American Racial Anglo-Saxonism*, Cambridge, Mass.: Harvard University Press.

Husband, C. (1982) 'Introduction: "Race", the Continuity of a Concept', in C. Husband (ed.) *'Race' in Britain: Continuity and Change*, London: Hutchinson.

Husbands, C. (1982) 'Contemporary Right-wing Extremism in Western European Democracies: A Review Article', *European Journal of Political Research*, 9: 75-99.

Huttenback, R.A. (1976) *Racism and Empire: White Settlers and Coloured Immigrants in the British Self-Governing Colonies 1830-1910*, Ithaca: Cornell University Press.

Huxley, J. and Haddon, A.C. (1935) *We Europeans: A Survey of 'Racial' Problems*, London: Cape.

Jenkins, R. (1986) *Racism and Recruitment: Managers, Organisations and Equal Opportunity in the Labour Market*, Cambridge: Cambridge University Press.

Jones, G. (1980) *Social Darwinism in English Thought: the Interaction Between Biological and Social Theory*, Brighton: Harvester Press.

Jones, J.S. (1981) 'How Different are Human Races?', *Nature*, 293: 188-90.

Jordan, W.J. (1968) *White Over Black: American Attitudes Toward the Negro, 1550-1812*, Chapel Hill: University of North Carolina Press.

Joshi, S. and Carter, B. (1984) 'The Role of Britain in the Creation of a Racist Britain', *Race and Class*, 25, 3: 53-70.

Kabbani, R. (1986) *Europe's Myth of Orient: Devise and Rule*, London: Macmillan.

Kamin, L.J. (1977) *The Science and Politics of I.Q.*, Harmondsworth: Penguin.

Katz, J.H. (1978) *White Awareness: Handbook for Anti-Racism Training*, Norman: University of Oklahoma Press.

Kaye, J. (1985) 'Islamic Imperialism and the Creation of Some Ideas of "Europe"', in F. Baker (ed.) *Europe and its Others*, vol. 1, Colchester: Essex University Press.

Kayyali, A.W. (ed.) (1979) *Zionism, Imperialism and Racism*, London: Croom Helm.

Kedourie, E. (1985) *Nationalism*, London: Hutchinson.

Kiernan, V. (1972) *The Lords of Human Kind: European Attitudes to the Outside World in the Imperial Age*, Harmondsworth: Penguin.

Kiewiet, C.W. de (1941) *A History of South Africa*, Oxford: Clarendon Press.

Knowles, L.L. and Prewitt, K. (1969) *Institutional Racism in America*, Englewood Cliffs: Prentice-Hall.

Kolchin, P. (1987) *Unfree Labour: American Slavery and Russian Serfdom*, London: Harvard University Press.

Krausnick, H., Buchheim, H., Broszat, M., and Jacobsen, H.A. (1968) *Anatomy of the SS State*, London: Collins.

Larrain, J. (1979) *The Concept of Ideology*, London: Hutchinson.

—— (1983) *Marxism and Ideology*, London: Macmillan.

Lecourt, D. (1980) 'Marxism as a Critique of Sociological Theories', in UNESCO *Sociological Theories: Race and Colonialism*, Paris: UNESCO.

Leech, K. (1986) '"Diverse Reports" and the Meaning of "Racism"', *Race and Class*, 28, 2: 82-8.

Lepervanche, M. de (1984) *Indians in a White Australia*, Sydney: Allen & Unwin.

—— (1987) 'Racism and Sexism in Australian National Identity', Mimeo paper read in Department of Sociology, University of Glasgow.

Levitas, R. (ed.) (1986) *The Ideology of the New Right*, London: Polity Press.

Levy, D.J. (1986) 'Here Be Witches! "Anti-Racism" and the Making of a New Inquisition', in F. Palmer (ed.) *Anti-Racism – An Assault on Education and Value*, London: Sherwood Press.

Lewis, B. (1971) *Race and Color in Islam*, New York: Harper Torchbooks.

—— (1982) *The Muslim Discovery of Europe*, London: Weidenfeld & Nicolson.

Liffman, M. (1985) 'Racism? What Do You Mean?', *Australian Society*, April: 29-31.

Lovejoy, A.O. (1936) *The Great Chain of Being: A Study of the History of an Idea*, Cambridge, Mass.: Harvard University Press.

Low, D.A. (1965) 'British East Africa: The Establishment of British Rule', in V. Harlow and E.M. Chiver (eds) *History of East Africa*, Vol. II, Oxford: Clarendon Press.

Lugard, F.D. (1929) *The Dual Mandate in British Tropical Africa*, Edinburgh: Blackwood.

Lukács, G. (1971) *History and Class Consciousness: Studies in Marxist Dialectics*, London: Merlin Press.

Macdonald, I.A. (1983) *Immigration Law and Practice in the United Kingdom*, London: Butterworths.

Macdonell, D. (1986) *Theories of Discourse: An Introduction*, Oxford: Basil Blackwell.

MacDougall, H.A. (1982) *Racial Myth in English History: Trojans, Teutons and Anglo-Saxons*, Montreal: Harvest House.

MacKenzie, J.M. (1984) *Propaganda and Empire: The Manipulation of British Public Opinion, 1880-1960*, Manchester: Manchester University Press.

McQueen, H. (1970) *A New Britannia: An Argument Concerning the Social Origins of Australian Radicalism and Nationalism*, Victoria: Penguin.

Mama, A. (1984) 'Black Women, the Economic Crisis and the British State', *Feminist Review*, 17: 21-35.

Marks, J. (1986) '"Anti-Racism" – Revolution not Education', in F. Palmer (ed.) *Anti-Racism – An Assault on Education and Value*, London: Sherwood Press.

Markus, A. and Ricklefs, M.C. (eds) (1985) *Surrender Australia? Essays in the Study and Uses of History*, Sydney: Allen & Unwin.

Marx, K. (1972) *Capital*, vol. 3, London: Lawrence & Wishart.

—— (1976) *Capital*, vol. 1, Harmondsworth: Penguin.

Maser, W. (1970) *Hitler's Mein Kampf: An Analysis*, London: Faber & Faber.

Mason, D. (1982) 'After Scarman: A Note on the Concept of Institutional Racism', *New Community*, 10, 1: 38-45.

Meillassoux, C. (1981) *Maidens, Meal and Money: Capitalism and the Domestic Community*, Cambridge: Cambridge University Press.

Miles, R. (1982) *Racism and Migrant Labour: A Critical Text*, London: Routledge & Kegan Paul.

—— (1984a) 'Marxism Versus the "Sociology of Race Relations"?', *Ethnic and Racial Studies*, 7, 2: 217-37.

—— (1984b) 'The Riots of 1958: The Ideological Construction of "Race Relations" as a Political Issue in Britain', *Immigrants and Minorities*, 3, 3: 252-75.

—— (1986) 'Labour Migration, Racism and Capital Accumulation in Western Europe Since 1945', *Capital and Class*, 28: 49-86.

—— (1987a) *Capitalism and Unfree Labour: Anomaly or Necessity?*, London: Tavistock.

—— (1987b) 'Class Relations and Racism in Britain in the 1980s', *Revue Européenne des Migrations Internationales*, 3, 1/2: 223-8.

—— (1987c) 'Recent Marxist Theories of Nationalism and the Issue of Racism', *British Journal of Sociology*, 38, 1: 24-43.

—— (1987d) 'Racism and Nationalism in Britain', in C. Husband (ed.) *'Race' in Britain: Continuity and Change*, London: Hutchinson.

—— (1988a) 'Beyond the "Race" Concept: The Reproduction of Racism in England', in M. de Lepervanche and G. Bottomley (eds) *The Cultural Construction of Race*, Sydney forthcoming.

—— (1988b) 'Marxism and the Idea of "Race"', *Leviathan*, forthcoming.

—— and Dunlop, A. (1986) 'The Racialisation of Politics in Britain: Why Scotland is Different', *Patterns of Prejudice*, 20, 1: 23-32.

—— and (1987) 'Racism in Britain: the Scottish Dimension', in P. Jackson (ed.) *Race and Racism*, London: George Allen & Unwin.

—— and Muirhead, L. (1986) 'Racism in Scotland: A Matter for Further Investigation', in D. McCrone (ed.) *Scottish Government Yearbook: 1986*, Edinburgh: Edinburgh University Press.

—— and Phizacklea, A. (1981) 'Racism and Capitalist Decline', in M. Harloe (ed.) *New Perspectives in Urban Change and Conflict*, London: Heinemann.

—— and Phizacklea, A. (1984) *White Man's Country: Racism in British Politics*, London: Pluto Press.

Mitter, S. (1986) 'Industrial Restructuring and Manufacturing Homework: Immigrant Women in the UK Clothing Industry', *Capital and Class*, 27: 37-80.

Montagu, A. (ed.) (1964) *The Concept of Race*, New York: Free Press.

—— (1972) *Statement on Race*, London: Oxford University Press.

—— (1974) *Man's Most Dangerous Myth: The Fallacy of Race*, New York: Oxford University Press.

Moscovici, S. (1981) 'On Social Representation', in J.P. Forgas (ed.) *Social Cognition: Perspectives on Everyday Understanding*, London: Academic Press.

—— (1982) 'The Coming Era of Representations', in J-P. Codol and J-P. Leyens (eds) *Cognitive Analysis of Social Behavior*, The Hague: Martinus Nijhoff.

—— (1984) 'The Phenomenon of Social Representations', in R.M. Farr and S. Moscovici (eds) *Social Representations*, Cambridge: Cambridge University Press.

Mosse, G.L. (1978) *Toward the Final Solution: A History of European Racism*, London: Dent & Sons.

Mungeam, G.H. (1966) *British Rule in Kenya: 1895-1912: The Establishment of Administration in the East Africa Protectorate*, Oxford: Clarendon Press.

Murray, N. (1986) 'Anti-racists and Other Demons: the Press and Ideology in Thatcher's Britain', *Race and Class*, 28, 3: 1-19.

Nairn, N.B. (1956) 'A Survey of the History of the White Australia Policy in the Nineteenth Century', *Australian Quarterly*, 28: 16-31.

Nairn, T. (1981) *The Break-Up of Britain*, London: Verso.

Nash, G.B. (1972) 'The Image of the Indian in the Southern Colonial Mind', in E. Dudley and M.E. Novak (eds) *The Wild Man Within: An Image in Western Thought from the Renaissance to Romanticism*, Pittsburgh: University of Pittsburgh Press.

Newnham, A. (1986) *Employment, Unemployment and Black People*, London: Runnymede Trust.

Nikolinakos, M. (1973) 'Notes on an Economic Theory of Racism', *Race*, 14, 4: 365-81.

Novak, M.E. (1972) 'The Wild Man Comes to Tea', in E. Dudley and M.E. Novak (eds) *The Wild Man Within: An Image in Western Thought from the Renaissance to Romanticism*, Pittsburgh: University of Pittsburgh Press.

Nowikowski, S. (1984) 'Snakes and Ladders: Asian Business in Britain', in R. Ward and R. Jenkins (eds) *Ethnic Communities in Business: Strategies for Economic Survival*, Cambridge: Cambridge University Press.

Oakley, A. (1981) *Subject Women*, Oxford: Martin Robertson.

Ogden, P. (1987) 'Immigration, Cities and the Geography of the National Front in France', in G. Glebe and J. O'Loughlin (eds) *Foreign Minorities in Continental European Cities*, Stuttgart: Franz Steiner Verlag Wiesbaden.

O'Keeffe, D.J. (1986) 'Preference and Prejudice: The Mythology of British Racism', in F. Palmer (ed.) *Anti-Racism – An Assault on Education and Value*, London: Sherwood Press.

Oliver, W.H. (ed.) (1981) *The Oxford History of New Zealand*, Wellington: Oxford University Press.

Omi, M. and Winant, H. (1986) *Racial Formation in the United States: From the 1960s to the 1980s*, New York: Routledge & Kegan Paul.

Palfreeman, A.C. (1972) 'The White Australia Policy', in F.S. Stevens (ed.) *Racism: The Australian Experience*, vol. 1: *Prejudice and Xenophobia*, New York: Taplinger Publishing Co.

Palmer, F. (ed.) (1986) *Anti-Racism – An Assault on Education and Value*, London: Sherwood Press.

Paludan, A. (1981) 'Refugees in Europe', *International Migration Review*, 15, 1/2: 69-73.

Peach, C. (1968) *West Indian Migration to Britain*, London: Oxford University Press.

Peukert, D.J.K. (1987) *Inside Nazi Germany: Conformity, Opposition and Racism in Everyday Life*, London: Batsford.

Phillips, D. (1987) 'The Rhetoric of Anti-Racism in Public Housing Allocation', in P. Jackson (ed.) *Race and Racism: Essays in Social Geography*, London: Allen & Unwin.

Phizacklea, A. and Miles, R. (1979) 'Working Class Racist Beliefs in the Inner City', in R. Miles and A. Phizacklea (eds) *Racism and Political Action in Britain*, London: Routledge & Kegan Paul.

—— (1980) *Labour and Racism*, London: Routledge & Kegan Paul.

Pinkney, A. (1976) *Red, Black, and Green: Black Nationalism in the United States*, Cambridge: Cambridge University Press.

—— (1984) *The Myth of Black Progress*, Cambridge: Cambridge University Press.

Poliakov, L. (1974) *The Aryan Myth: A History of Racist and Nationalist Ideas in Europe*, London: Heinemann.

Popkin, R.H. (1974) 'The Philosophical Basis of Modern Racism', in C. Walton and J.P. Anton (eds) *Philosophy and the Civilising Arts*, Athens: Ohio University Press.

Potter, J. and Wetherell, M. (1987) *Discourse and Social Psychology: Beyond Attitudes and Behaviour*, London: Sage.

Powell, E.J. (1969) *Freedom and Reality*, Kingswood: Paperfronts.

—— (1972) *Still to Decide*, Kingswood: Paperfronts.

Puzzo, D.A. (1964) 'Racism and the Western Tradition', *Journal of the History of Ideas*, 25, 4: 579-86.

Reeves, F. (1983) *British Racial Discourse: A Study of British Political Discourse About Race and Race-Related Matters*, Cambridge: Cambridge University Press.

Rex, J. (1970) *Race Relations in Sociological Theory*, London: Weidenfeld & Nicolson.

—— (1986) *Race and Ethnicity*, Milton Keynes: Open University Press.

—— and Tomlinson, S. (1979) *Colonial Immigrants in a British City: A Class Analysis*, London: Routledge & Kegan Paul.

Reynolds, H. (1972) *Aborigines and Settlers: the Australian Experience*, Melbourne: Cassell Australia Ltd.

Rich, P.B. (1986) *Race and Empire in British Politics*, Cambridge: Cambridge University Press.

Ripley, W.Z. (1900) *The Races of Europe: A Sociological Study*, London: Kegan Paul, Trench, Trübner & Co.

Robe, S.L. (1972) 'Wild Men and Spain's Brave New World', in E. Dudley and M.E. Novak (eds) *The Wild Man Within: An Image in Western Thought from the Renaissance to Romanticism*, Pittsburgh: University of Pittsburgh Press.

Robinson, C.J. (1983) *Black Marxism*, London: Zed Press.

Rose, S., Kamin, L.J., and Lewontin, R.C. (1984) *Not In Our Genes: Biology,*

Ideology and Human Nature, Harmondsworth: Penguin.

Rowley, C.D. (1970) *The Destruction of Aboriginal Society*, Canberra: Australian National University Press.

Said, E.W. (1985) *Orientalism*, Harmondsworth: Penguin.

Sanders, R. (1978) *Lost Tribes and Promised Lands: The Origins of American Racism*, Boston: Little, Brown and Co.

Saunders, K. (1982) *Workers in Bondage: The Origins and Bases of Unfree Labour in Queensland, 1824-1916*, St. Lucia: University of Queensland Press.

Sayer, D. (1979) *Marx's Method: Ideology, Science and Critique in 'Capital'*, Brighton: Harvester Press.

—— (1987) *The Violence of Abstraction: The Analytical Foundations of Historical Materialism*, Oxford: Basil Blackwell.

Schoen, D.E. (1977) *Enoch Powell and the Powellites*, London: Macmillan.

Seale, B. (1970) *Seize the Time: The Story of the Black Panther Party*, London: Arrow Books.

Searle, C. (1987) 'Your Daily Dose: Racism and the *Sun*', *Race and Class*, 29, 1: 55-71.

Seidel, G. (1986) *The Holocaust Denial: Antisemitism, Racism and the New Right*, Leeds: Beyond the Pale Collective.

Sender, J. and Smith, S. (1986) *The Development of Capitalism in Africa*, London: Methuen.

Seton-Watson, H. (1977) *Nations and States: An Enquiry into the Origins of Nations and the Politics of Nationalism*, London: Methuen.

Sitkoff, H. (1981) *The Struggle for Black Equality, 1954-1980*, New York: Hill & Wang.

Sivanandan, A. (1973) 'Race, Class and Power: An Outline for Study', *Race*, 14, 4: 383-91.

—— (1982) *A Different Hunger: Writings on Black Resistance*, London: Pluto Press.

—— (1983) 'Challenging Racism: Strategies for the '80s', *Race and Class*, 25, 2: 1-12.

—— (1985) 'RAT and the Degradation of the Black Struggle', *Race and Class*, 26, 4: 1-34.

Smith, A.D. (1983) *Theories of Nationalism*, London: Duckworth.

Smith, D.J. (1977) *Racial Disadvantage in Britain*, Harmondsworth: Penguin.

—— (1981) *Unemployment and Racial Minorities*, London: Policy Studies Institute.

—— (1983) *Police and People in London, III: A Survey of Police Officers*, London: Policy Studies Institute.

Smithies, B. and Fiddick, P. (1969) *Enoch Powell on Immigration*, London: Sphere Books.

Snowden, F.M. (1970) *Blacks in Antiquity: Ethiopians in the Greco-Roman Experience*, Cambridge, Mass.: Harvard University Press.

—— (1983) *Before Colour Prejudice: the Ancient View of Blacks*, Cambridge, Mass.: Harvard University Press.

Sorrenson, M.P.K. (1965) 'Land Policy in Kenya, 1895-1945', in V. Harlow and E.M. Chiver (eds) *History of East Africa*, vol. II, Oxford: Clarendon Press.

—— (1968) *Origins of European Settlement in Kenya*, Nairobi: Oxford University Press.

Southern, R.W. (1962) *Western Views of Islam in the Middle Ages*, Cambridge, Mass.: Harvard University Press.

Stanton, W. (1960) *The Leopard's Spots: Scientific Attitudes Toward Race in America, 1815-59*, Chicago: University of Chicago Press.

Stepan, N. (1982) *The Idea of Race in Science: Great Britain 1800-1960*, London: Macmillan.

Stichter, S. (1982) *Migrant Labour in Kenya: Capitalism and African Response 1895-1975*, London: Longman.

Stocking, G.W. (1968) *Race, Culture and Evolution*, New York: Free Press.

Street, B.V. (1975) *The Savage in Literature*, London: Routledge & Kegan Paul.

Symcox, G. (1972) 'The Wild Man's Return: The Enclosed Vision of Rousseau's Discourses', in E. Dudley and M.E. Novak (eds) *The Wild Man Within: An Image in Western Thought from the Renaissance to Romanticism*, Pittsburgh: University of Pittsburgh Press.

Tambs-Lyche, H. (1980) *London Patidars: A Case Study of Urban Ethnicity*, London: Routledge & Kegan Paul.

Taylor, S. (1982) *The National Front in English Politics*, London: Macmillan.

Temperley, H. (1972) *British Anti-Slavery 1833-1870*, London: Longman.

Thornton, A.P. (1965) *Doctrines of Imperialism*, New York: Wiley.

Thurlow, R.C. (1980) 'Satan and Sambo: the Image of the Immigrant in English Racial Populist Thought Since the First World War', in K. Lunn (ed.) *Hosts, Immigrants and Minorities: Historical Responses to Newcomers in British Society 1870-1914*, Folkestone: Dawson.

Tignor, R.L. (1976) *The Colonial Transformation of Kenya: The Kambu, Kikuyu, and Masai from 1900 to 1939*, Princeton: Princeton University Press.

Trigger, B.G. (1985) *Natives and Newcomers: Canada's 'Heroic Age' Reconsidered*, Kingston/Montreal: McGill-Queen's University Press.

Troyna, B. and Williams, J. (1985) *Racism, Education and the State: The Racialisation of Education Policy*, London: Croom Helm

Twaddle, M. (1975) *Expulsion of a Minority: Essays on Ugandan Asians*, London: Athlone Press.

Unit for Manpower Studies (1977) *The Role of Immigrants in the Labour Market*, London: Department of Employment.

Van den Berghe, P.L. (1978) *Race and Racism: A Comparative Perspective*, New York: Wiley.

Volkenkundig Museum Nusantara (1986) *Met Andere Ogen: 400 Jaar Afbeeldingen van Europeanen Door Verre Volken*, Delft: Volkenkundig Museum Nusantara.

Walker, M. (1977) *The National Front*, London: Fontana.

Wallerstein, I. (1974) *The Modern World System I: Capitalist Agriculture and the Origins of the European World Economy in the Sixteenth Century*, New York: Academic Press.

—— (1983) *Historical Capitalism*, London: Verso.

Walvin, J. (1973) *Black and White: The Negro and English Society 1555-1945*, London: Allen Lane.

—— (1986) *England, Slaves and Freedom, 1776-1838*, London: Macmillan.

Wellman, D. (1977) *Portraits of White Racism*, Cambridge: Cambridge University Press.

Werbner, P. (1984) 'Pakistani Entrepreneurship in the Manchester Garment Trade', in R. Ward and R. Jenkins (eds) *Ethnic Communities in Business: Strategies for Survival*, Cambridge: Cambridge University Press.

White, H. (1972) 'The Forms of Wildness: Archaeology of an Idea', in E. Dudley and M.E. Novak (eds) *The Wild Man Within: An Image in Western Thought from the Renaissance to Romanticism*, Pittsburg: University of Pittsburg Press.

Wihtol de Wenden, C. (1987) 'France's Policy on Migration from May 1981 till March 1986: Its Symbolic Dimension, Its Restrictive Aspects and its Unintended Effects', *International Migration*, 25, 2: 211-19.

Willard, M. (1967) *History of the White Australia Policy to 1920*, Melbourne: Melbourne University Press.

Williams, E. (1964) *Capitalism and Slavery*, London: Deutsch.

Williams, J. (1985) 'Redefining Institutional Racism', *Ethnic and Racial Studies*, 8, 3: 323-48.

Wilson, D. (1978) 'Asian Entrepreneurs: From High Street to Park Lane', *The Director*, June: 30-2.

Wolf, E. (1982) *Europe and the People Without History*, Berkeley: University of California Press.

Wolpe, H. (1980) 'Capitalism and Cheap Labour Power in South Africa: From Segregation to Apartheid', in H. Wolpe (ed.) *The Articulation of Modes of Production*, London: Routledge & Kegan Paul.

Wright, P. (1968) *The Coloured Worker in British Industry*, Oxford: Oxford University Press.

Wright, P. (1985) *On Living in an Old Country*, London: Verso.

Wrigley, C.C. (1965) 'Kenya: The Pattern of Economic Life, 1902-1945', in V. Harlow and E.M. Chiver (eds) *History of East Africa*, vol. II, Oxford: Clarendon Press.

Yarwood, A.T. (1962) 'The "White Australia" Policy: A Reinterpretation of its Development in the Late Colonial Period', *Historical Studies*, 10: 257-69.

—— (1964) *Asian Migration to Australia: The Background to Exclusion 1896-1939*, Melbourne: Melbourne University Press.

Yuval-Davies, N. (1986) 'Ethnic/Racial Divisions and the Nation in Britain and Australia', *Capital and Class*, 28: 87-103.

Index